D0100085

MULIEBRITY:

Qualities of a Woman

Joni Arredia

MULIEBRITY:
Qualities of a Woman

Perc Publishing • Toledo, Ohio

ISBN 0-9653203-1-6
Library of Congress Catalog Number 96-092493

Cover, endleaves, and illustrations by
Kevin Ewing, Ewing Design and Illustration
Interior by Troy Scott Parker, Cimarron Design

Perc Publishing, 5019 Dauber Drive West, Toledo, Ohio 43615
PERC: Personal Energies, Resources, and Capabilities

To those around whom my whole world revolves:

Ylime, Nerual, and Kcuhc.

You are the "wind beneath my wings."

Who loves ya, Sweetie?

Ymmom, Naoj.

Acknowledgments

HUGS AND KISSES ALWAYS to my dear, sweet, little family for all you have taught me. The love you give me nourishes me and gives me the strength to reach for the stars. That is the greatest love of all.

Thanks to Barbara Stahl, my producer, for her constant encouragement, patience and love. You were there from the beginning, and I only hope and pray you'll be there to the very, very end. The fun has just started.

Dear Barb Meyer, my editor. Our pebbled road is smooth as silk now. Thank you for sharing with me all the blood, sweat and tears. I could never deny that you made my words come alive.

Loving Anne Crowley. Yes Anne, we are traveling kindred spirits and I cherish our adventures more than you'll ever know.

Paula Tscholl and R.M. Tscholl; Patty Loizou; Buddy, Maryann and Alyson Ray; Dee Isaac; Colleen Langenderfer; Deb Jernigan;

Maureen, Megan and Darrah Carr; Shirley Hollstein; Susie Shew; Jane Charette; Mary Lynn Valdes Dapena; and Jodi Stamp: Thank you, thank you, thank you for your candid thoughts. You all had the very first glimpse of the manuscript—and still loved me. Ditto!

And to all the Perfect Strangers/Perfect Friends in my life: *Hats off to you!*

Contents

Your inner beauty

Smile!

Reveal your inner beauty for the outer edge

for the outer edge

MULIEBRITY

Qualities of a Woman

A MAGIC

CARPET RIDE

I AM WRITING THIS BOOK BECAUSE I HAVE A QUESTION to ask women. A profound question, as in "Why can't we all be happy?" I mean truly comfortable in our own skin, beautiful in our own eyes as well as in the eyes of others.

The fact is, we most definitely can be!

I know that's true, because I've done it myself, and I'm writing this book as a way of sharing the process—my magic carpet ride—with you.

In many ways, that process, and this book, have been forty years in the making. But in others—the ways that seem to count the most—that journey is only four years old.

Four years ago, I took control of my life. Oh, my friends, it was the toughest thing to do. But the freedom

I gained was immeasurable. I got rid of the garbage that weighed me down in the past. I grabbed that monkey off my back, locked it in a cage, and threw the key down the biggest, deepest black hole. And I vowed to myself never to look down that hole again.

There's a song by Whitney Houston titled "One Moment in Time." It imparts strength, gives us the feeling that we can conquer the world. That's good, because we can. But it also suggests that there is only one moment, one mesmerizing, unbelievable moment in which we can.

No way!

There are trillions of those moments in time. That's something else I learned on my magic carpet ride, because before I started it, I had decided to enjoy every minute of life, fill my cup full, and let it overflow with joy to those around me.

On my journey, I figured out many things; in writing this book, I figured out many, many more, both for you and for me. I was as kind and strong and giving and powerful as I possibly could be while I wrote for us.

My prayer is that when all is said and done, you, too, will be kind, strong, giving and powerful. That sums up being a woman who has maximized her potential, explored the glories of being female.

Keep in mind that my book is not one of those one-formula-fits-all self-help books. I read several of those getting ready to write for us, and I know that we don't need another one. We need a feel-good-about-how-wonderful-it-is-to-be-female book. A book that will inspire us to believe that, to achieve that, and share it with our mothers, our daughters, our sisters, our friends.

So I have written a volume that encourages us, not to "paint by the numbers," but rather to explore and outline the outer edges of our very personal dreams, then ever so softly color in the varied shades of inner beauty that can make those dreams come true and happiness an ever-present reality.

A short time ago, I came upon a fabulous word that was new to me: *muliebrity*. It's defined as "the state of being a woman," "the qualities characteristic of women," or "possessing full womanly powers." Together, we're going to talk about many of those qualities and powers, and how they can help us on our personal journey to happiness and maximized potential. We'll also talk about the baggage we should discard to lighten our load along the way.

So hop on my magic carpet, and let's get started!

WE'VE ALL GOT

HISTORY

To live in fear as a small child is to gain incredible insight as an adult.

I HAVE HAD THE RUNS all morning, getting ready to remember those years I have tried so hard to forget. I went rollerblading this morning in twenty-one-degree weather to gather the strength to pull all those dreadful memories up to the forefront of my mind.

It was so much easier to write every other bit of this book because each represents a part of what I have become, a point I always dreamed of reaching. Those dreams made me the survivor I am today.

As much as I would rather not write this chapter, unless I write it, the rest of this book may not make any sense to you.

This book talks about being comfortable in our own skin, being the best we can be: it's not just the good things that have happened to us that help us learn to do that. The bad things can play a pivotal role if we come to terms with them, and use what we learned in the process of surviving them. But that doesn't just happen: those bad things have to be addressed, and addressing them directly was the most painful part of my own magic carpet ride.

I'm going to tell you about my bad things in this chapter because I think it's important that you understand where I came from to get to where I am today. Your bad things may be very different, but maybe, just maybe, this chapter will help you address the bad things in your own life and move ever closer to your dreams.

**I never smiled as a child.
It was always a problem in pictures.
People would do everything they could
to get me to smile.**

Funny enough, I believed I was smiling—until I saw the actual photographs. I *thought* I was turning up my lips. Not until decades later would I understand why I didn't smile.

Our younger daughter, Miss Em, was about six years old when she asked me, "Mommy, why weren't you smiling in any of your pictures when you were little?"

Just like that, memories came back to me. Flooding back, breaking through the mental barriers I'd erected to block them out.

Oh, the innocence of children: it had all been stripped from me. "Emily," I said, "Mommy wasn't happy when she was a little girl."

This is where it gets tough, so stick with me. As much as I have used writing to help me deal with my past, I have never before put this on paper.

I was a product—I am a product—of child sexual abuse.

My fear about writing about what happened to me is that it's been written about so much lately, and I don't want to bore you. But for you to really understand the attitude I possess now with true ownership and pride, you must understand the little girl I was back then. I earned this incredible attitude, the same as I know you already have, or soon will, perhaps with the help of this book.

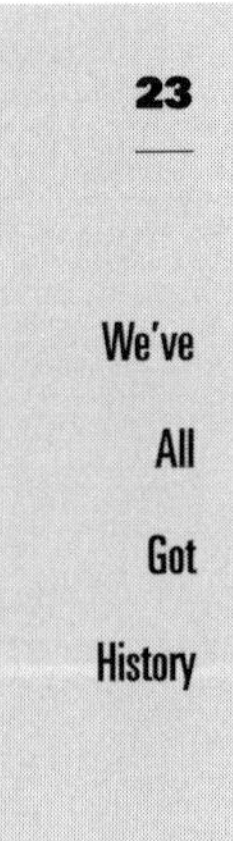

That Boy.
I hated him.
I feared him.
&
And I loved him.

You may wonder who That Boy was. But, you know, it doesn't really matter, because this book is not about finger-pointing: it's about getting on with our lives. So suffice it to say that he was a boy, somewhat older than I, whom my family loved and trusted completely. He was in and out of our house—and our lives—throughout my childhood.

That Boy played upon my shyness and insecurities. He knew I was frail in spirit, and he fed upon that. He was a vampire who sucked all the life out of me for five or six long years, starting when I was just four years old. Long time, long time, much too long.

He pretended to love me and shield me from the world. He "understood" me. And as he loved, and understood, and shielded, he expected payment in return. It was a nonverbal agreement. I was young, too young, too little to know any better. Everyone in my family loved him and trusted him, so I did, too.

What could a four-year-old possibly know in 1959? The entertainment we saw was as innocent as I was: we were watching *Ozzie and Harriet,* not the *Movie of the Week.* It was a time when we were all sheltered from sex, violence, divorce, gangs, and dirty laundry hung out for the whole world to see. The only laundry being hung on the line was what we wore.

You wonder why my parents never knew what was going on. People back then didn't think in those terms, didn't talk to little children about not letting people touch them intimately.

What That Boy was doing to me would have been inconceivable to my parents.

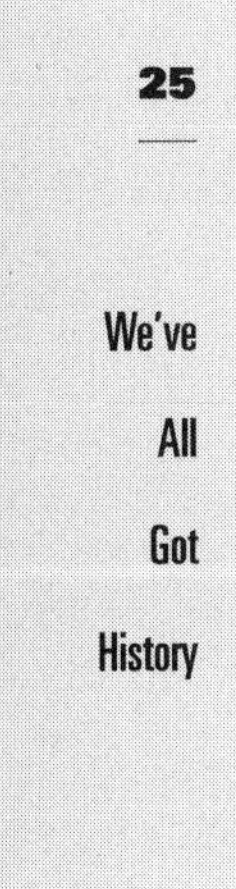

Mom and Dad had seven children quickly, no birth control. Not as Catholics. A good Catholic woman in the Fifties had as many children as God sent.

So the babies kept coming, and our home grew more chaotic with each new sibling. Dad was busy working to feed all those children. He was moving up in his career, which meant long hours at the office, away from his family.

Can you see how awareness on their part might get lost in the shuffle of life?

My life.

When I was real little That Boy would take me to his hideaway places, just the two of us. He'd make me feel special: just me and him. He knew what to say and how to hold my hand. I felt wanted, secure, not so painfully shy. We would undress. (My family loved him, so it was okay, right?) Then he would lie on his back and I would straddle him and urinate all over him, because he told me to. Sick. Unfortunately, that was only the beginning.

(But my family loved him, so it was okay, right?)

When I was in kindergarten and first grade, I used to play sick all the time. As a matter of fact, I got pretty good at it. When I pretended to be sick, I could stay home: That Boy couldn't get me if he was in school all day and I was home. Just me and Mom. No fears. A bit of undivided attention. Alone. Nobody to touch me or tell me to touch him.

I loved those days at home. Dry toast and tea, no sugar. In my jammies all day, watching TV, believing that I was going to be in that picture tube one day, the star. The *untouchable* star. Beautiful and smiling. In charge of every situation, and I mean every. Boys asking for dates, and me, turning them away. I lived for the times when I could get lost in the afternoon movie and picture myself as the star.

As I sit at my keyboard writing this,
my hands are shaking. As I gaze out my window,
the falling snow is soft and light and peaceful,
just like in a glass Christmas snowball ornament.
You know, the kind you shake up to create a
perfect, happy setting for life. The life as a child
I so longed to hold in my little hands.

Why was That Boy so tender to me at times, only to set me up for the struggle to come? I could see in his eyes when the time was near for more touching and getaway places to hide. It was a look of longing and trouble, and, to me, utterly disgusting. That look came to represent deception and exploitation.

To this day, I can spot it in a person's eyes. My instincts are so incredibly strong now. My senses are keenly aware. Whenever anyone is too nice—as **he** was at first before the touching—I am sure he wants something.

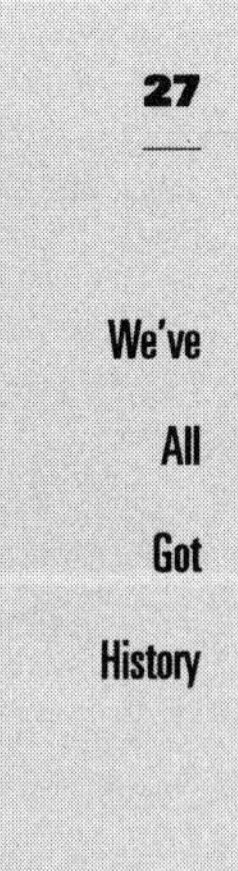

As much as I prayed the ugliness would stop, it didn't.

We lived on a river when I was a child, just a block or two from the county orphanage. I used to go there and talk to the kids through the fence. We had so much in common: they wanted to be free, and so did I. Their fence was physical; mine was invisible, but just as imprisoning.

I longed to trade places with those orphans, just to escape the touching. I dreamed of being in their shoes. But there was one drawback: I couldn't take my parents with me. Even at that age, with all the terribleness, I had my parents, and I wouldn't have traded them for anything, especially my father.

There were many tender moments in my childhood, and most of them were spent with Dad.

Dad had a way of unconditionally holding me and stroking my hair that always made me feel safe and secure. When I was little and we took a drive together, I would lay my head on his lap and look out the window at the sun or the stars and feel happier than I could ever have imagined.

When bad things happened, I longed for the safe haven of my father's car.

One morning when I was quite young, Dad and I were tickling and wrestling in his bed. How I was giggling and loving it, bathing in the delight of it all! Then Mom came in and was very mad that we were behaving that way, or the way she thought we might be. I knew immediately what she was thinking: she thought maybe it was all too warm and fuzzy for a grown-man-daddy and a young-girl-daughter to be frolicking under the covers.

"He isn't That Boy," I wanted to scream. "Daddy has never made me do things like that. Daddy really, truly loves me."

Sadly, although there was nothing whatsoever wrong in what he was doing, Daddy never frolicked with me like that again. Never. More of that innocence removed. Was I to worry about all men that way for the rest of my life? Had I nothing to look forward to now? But Dad still let me lay my head on his lap, and he still stroked my hair.

Dad's sweetness helped me through the rough spots. Despite the abuse, I knew then, because of my father, that there were good men I could believe in. To this day, when things get tough, I long to sit next to him and have him play with my hair: then I'd know that all was right in my world.

Then there was my dear, sweet sister, Frannie, "Frannie Wan," just seventeen months younger than I. She had an easier time making friends than I did, and she always included me. When we were young, sometimes Frannie and I walked to Woolworth's, then went our separate ways in the store to spend our precious fifty cents on each other. We'd meet outside on the curb with our little shopping bags and exchange our thoughtful, beautiful goodies. Just me and Frannie.

My memories of this are so vivid and full of love: I was learning the art of giving from my heart and soul from my younger sister. It was unconditional giving, and it felt wonderful, especially to a little girl who had been a victim of unconditional taking.

At the time, I thought Frannie had no idea of the horror I was dealing with. I just figured she had an inkling that something wasn't quite right, and had decided to shelter me under her wing. Not until many, many years later did I learn that she, too, was That Boy's victim. And in her pain, she reached out to be my guardian angel.

So Daddy and Frannie Wan made life bearable. Living on the river was also a Godsend. It became home for me. I could go there often, and sing, and just be. I had my own secret hiding place where no one could find me. I became very good at being hidden and quiet. Someone could walk a foot in front of me and never hear or see me. It was a terrific game, one where I was in total charge.

On the riverbank, I played out my roles of stardom. Fantasy became my best friend. I was the daydreamer of all daydreamers. I remember being yelled at for all that daydreaming. "Get your head out of the clouds," they would say. But my mind was my sanctuary. No one could enter without my permission. It belonged only to me. I had complete ownership.

Down by the river, I first became aware of the beauties of nature. I made lots of animal friends who came to the river to feed. I found little, scared, injured animals, nursed them back to health, then set them free with all my love. I was most fond of baby birds, because when they healed, they could fly far, far away. "Please, teach me to fly; take me with you," I'd say to them. In my dreams as a child I was always flying: it was the fastest way out. A magic carpet ride.

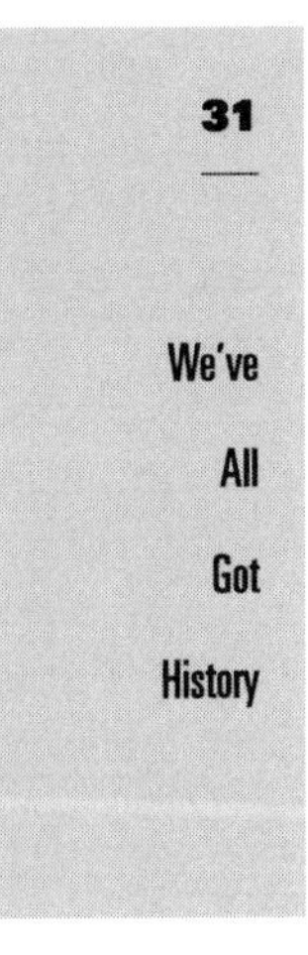

But the riverbank was also That Boy's feeding ground—of a much different kind. There were so many trees and bushes he could lurk behind and take me unawares. I was getting older: six, seven, eight, wanting more than ever for this to stop. He was getting stronger and fiercer towards my resistance, no longer initiating contact in a tender way. It was as though I was only an object to which he was addicted. He became more and more like a vicious animal who receives pleasure from the kill, but who also requires more variety in each new kill in order to be satisfied.

He was a very mean boy, and so I did what he wanted, even though I didn't want to.

"This is our secret; don't ever tell, or I'll kill you," That Boy threatened. And so I never told.

One warm summer evening, my family and I had walked to the park to watch some boys, including **him,** play softball. When it was his turn at bat, he told us all to stay down, in fact, practically lie down. But at the ripe old age of four or five, I had ants in my pants, and I didn't want to get down. I already was sick and tired of being a slave to That Boy's whims.

So I stood up at precisely the moment he swung the hard wooden baseball bat—crack, right into my face. He yelled, "I told you to stay down." To this day, I'm not sure if that whole episode was a power struggle or merely an accident. But my fear of him intensified. And when he said he'd kill me if I told, I believed him.

That Boy had fiery eyes that said he meant business. Once you've been transfixed by those eyes you know there's no way out, and you better play along or God forbid what could happen. I saw his temper with others, and it wasn't pretty. He was a bully, and I'd already felt his wrath.

To add to my trauma, I was held back in the second grade. I hated school. I wanted to be home with my mother, playing sick and being loved and nurtured. He wasn't able to bother me then.

My parents thought I was failing because my November birthday meant I started school too young, and I simply wasn't ready. But I was ready. I was just afraid of people. I thought for sure that they all knew what was happening with That Boy. I couldn't concentrate.

I wanted to be home, tucked in the safety of Mom and Dad's bed, watching all the old Fred Astaire-Ginger Rogers musicals that seemed to be on nearly every afternoon in those days, dreaming of the day I would be a star. That untouchable star.

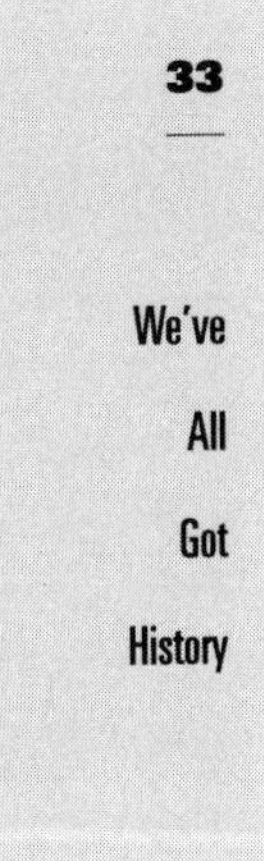

To return to the same school and the same classroom to repeat second grade was horrifying. I was in tears the first morning. As I walked past the third-grade classroom with all the kids from my class the year before, I cringed, and they snickered. The things That Boy was doing to me made it hard enough to look anyone in the eye. Now I had lost all face by failing second grade.

Then, when I looked into the window of the second grade classroom, I froze. Those kids would never like me: flunking meant I was stupid and That Boy had told me over and over again that I was an ugly duckling. Ugly and stupid meant I wouldn't have friends.

I was right: there were no friends that school year. I remember absolutely nothing of that second second-grade year, except the reverberation of cruel young voices calling me "Flunky."

Sexual abuse. Failure. Fear.
And a few treasured moments of happiness.
That was my childhood.
Certainly less than ideal.

But I've come to realize that it was hardly unique, and certainly not an excuse for failing to get my act together decades later.

I have a friend who says it so well: "We've all got history." She said it the first time after getting off the phone with a woman who was going on for the zillionth time about how terrible her childhood was and that was why she couldn't fall in love, find the right job, *etc., etc., etc.* You know the routine; you may have even done it yourself.

I hope you know by now that I would be the last person on earth to diminish the fact that many of us have been victims of terrible acts in childhood, even adulthood. Sexual, physical, emotional abuse. Neglect. Parental and spousal selfishness and insensitivity. I could go on all day and still not complete that horrific list: over the years, I've talked to women whose pasts make mine look like a Sunday School picnic.

But once victims, why do we allow ourselves to remain victims of the past throughout our lives? Why do we allow those who controlled us so cruelly in the past to continue to control us now—even though they are no longer a part of our lives? Why do we let them stand between us and happiness?

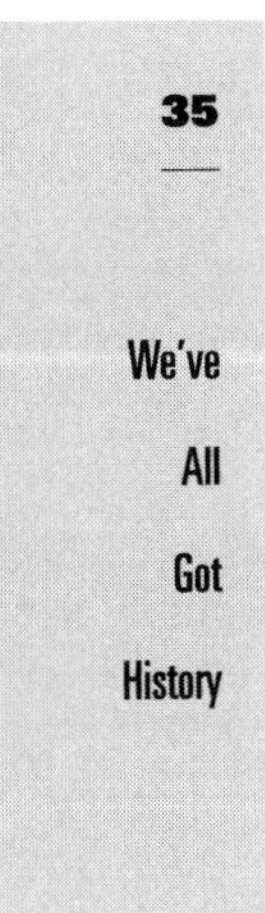

No matter how heartbreaking the damage done to us, we have to come to terms with it, and then we have to triumph over it. And how do we achieve that victory? By using what we learned—and trust me, we learned lots—to live the lives we want to lead from this day forward.

Some of us retreat into our imaginations as a result of our childhood problems. Others learn to be all things to all people. There are dozens and dozens of ways we adapt to shield our hearts and bodies from pain. So why not take those abilities—once defense mechanisms—and use them to become whatever and whomever we want to be?

Because of what I experienced as a child,
I possess an almost supernatural ability
to be atuned to,
to intuit the thoughts of,
every person with whom I come in contact.

I don't like the way I acquired that ability,
but the fact is that I earned it,
and I'm going to put it to use
to help me achieve what I want in life.

As a result of my childhood, I have an immeasurable amount of love and sensitivity towards others. An understanding. It's my trademark.

It began on the riverbank where I cared for small, injured animals. Later, in high school, it bloomed fully when I volunteered at the State Hospital in order to earn school credits. This was in the early 1970s.

The hospital was designed to house people with mental problems. Once a week, my school friends and I drove onto the grounds, first seeing the adult house with its tower, its residents screaming and shaking the bars on the windows. That brought tears to my eyes every week: pretty nerve-racking stuff for a sixteen-year-old—or maybe no matter what your age.

I was enlisted to help in the hospital's Teen House where I met kids just like me, my peers—except they were locked up and given drugs to calm them, balance them, keep them orderly. They didn't need those drugs. For the most part, they were just kids who came from broken homes: their parents didn't know what to do with them, so they stuck them in a mental hospital. But those poor kids weren't crazy: they were simply enraged at their fate.

A handful of us went to work at the Teen House, charged with spending time—happy time—with those kids, and cleaning up their environment. Together, we painted, cleaned, and spruced up the place. The best part, however, was that we all, volunteers and residents, ended up working as a team. Believe me, it didn't start that way.

At first, those kids weren't happy about our invading their territory. They were very skeptical, and I can't say that I blame them. But we slowly earned their trust, and after a few months the house was done. We decided to throw a party to celebrate: most of the residents had never had a party before. We made food, scrounged up a phonograph, and brought records from home. Everyone was all worked up by the time party day arrived.

But that was a sad day, too. You see, it was to be our last day with the residents. And although we didn't have the heart to tell them, they knew it—instinctively. We'd become such friends: we volunteers were once-a-week normalcy in their lives. And for me, the residents were a reality check. They were behind locked doors with their problems. But I, I was walking around free of external restraints, but inside lay my locked doors, hiding the horror that had festered and grown since I was four years old. (Although the abuse had ended by then, I hadn't yet fully faced the reality of what it had done to me.)

I know the residents of Teen House felt we'd betrayed them by leaving: the problem was that I needed them as much as they needed me. I wanted to go back even though my school requirement was fulfilled. But the nurse at Teen House asked me not to: the kids I'd learned to love made a turn for the worse when we left. They'd felt, once again, abandoned by someone they trusted. I continue to pray that each found a lick of luck and is as happy and fulfilled as we all were the day of our party.

First the wounded animals, then these wounded kids: I discovered that being a victim as a child gave me a sensitivity to others in pain. And with those kids in Teen House, I realized that we all have a sweetness about us that no amount of ugliness done to us could erase.

It has been said,
"Whatever doesn't kill me makes me stronger."
Used constructively,
this thought has helped me shape the life
I want to live.

What abilities did your childhood give you? Right now, make a mental list. Are you sensitive to others? Can you tell when your spouse or child or mother or friend is quietly suffering? Did you develop a sense of humor to deal with life's difficulties? Perhaps you're a take-charge person who helps others deal with life at its most overwhelming. Or a nurturer, as so many of us women tend to be. So tell me, what did you learn?

My childhood gave me the ability to find a ray of sunshine beyond a dark cloud. I sensed when others needed that ray, too, and I learned to help them find it, if only for a moment. I also learned that I was no better than anyone else, and that no one else was better than I was, because we'd all been dealt a bad hand of cards at some point in our short lives.

I learned that my feet and my imagination could take me wherever I dare to go. Mostly, I learned that to be nice is the only way to live.

I'm not going to lie to you: coming to terms with the past may be the most painful thing you've ever done, and it may take some time. It may require you to dig deep, remember things you'd rather not, and trust a friend or lover or professional good listener to help you on this journey. And the path of your journey may not follow the course mine took.

But once you've dealt with it, *you* have control of the pain and the past: they no longer control you. And a good part of gaining that control is using what you learned during your past to help you become the woman you want to be. The greatness of coming to terms with your past is that you know you will never allow it to be repeated again.

I've written this book to help you think about ways you can gain that control. And I know it can be done because I did it. So, as we continue through this book, start to think how you can use those hard-won abilities—those qualities that contribute to muliebrity—to achieve your dreams, maximize your potential as a woman, and become truly happy.

A ROADMAP

OF MY JOURNEY

MY JOURNEY TO HAPPINESS started when I was little, when the abuse was still going on. At the time, I had no idea I'd started down my path to fulfillment: I simply knew that if I ran fast enough and far enough, That Boy couldn't catch me. Now I recognize that the first step on that path was movement, exercise, a sense of control over my own body that in later years extended to eating right, practicing good nutrition.

Soon after I began to revel in movement, I recognized that people responded positively if I did good things. And so I trained myself to be of service to others, because their reactions fed my soul, something the ugliness and negativity I harbored inside as a result of being abused could never do.

I also realized that if I looked good, people treated me as though I were pretty. And so I learned to dress well, because I wanted that reaction. As I mentioned, all the time That Boy abused me, he told me I was an ugly duckling, and I believed him. So while I couldn't completely accept compliments as true, I hungered for them.

Developing these external attributes—movement, service to others, dress—did several positive things for me in the first thirty-some years of my journey.

They caused others to treat me like I was a good person. Only I knew how ugly and ashamed I really was. Developing my externals was like forging a beautiful armor around me so no one could really see all the ugliness inside.

Those externals did provide me with a kind of happiness. Certainly not the complete happiness I know now, but a happiness I'd never experienced before. With exercise and eating right and good deeds and dress in place, my life went fairly well for three decades. To the extent I was capable, I was happy.

I also know now that concentrating on externals kept me from thinking about what had been done to me when I was young. And that, in fact, was a good thing.

Our society's talk-show-let's-explore-the-psychological-horror mentality often ignores a very basic truth: sometimes we simply aren't ready to take a look at our worst demons. Sometimes we must focus on what we **can** do until we're strong enough to face our most difficult issues. For some folks, those demons are internal issues; for others, they're the very externals that came first for me. We are all individuals, and we must each start our journey with the steps that are most natural to us: when it's time to take the big steps, we'll know it, and all we've done before will have prepared us to handle them.

That Boy stopped abusing me when I was ten years old. Even as a small child, I loved to pray, and prayer gave me the strength to finally tell Mom and Dad what he was doing to me. Thank God, they believed me, and the abuse came to an abrupt and welcome end. But its effects lingered on, hidden deep inside till the time I could handle them.

That time came not long after my little Emily asked why I never smiled.

As I told you, memories flooded back when she asked that question—but not all of them—and, to my surprise, I didn't fall apart completely. The confidence I'd gained through developing externals held me steady. Then, just a short time later, I finally met the challenge of confronting the past head on.

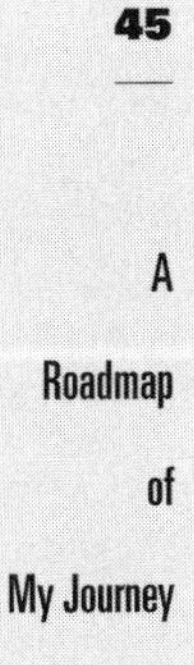

Four years ago, family and friends were pitching in financially to deal with some trials and tribulations some other members of my family were facing. That Boy needed some help before he could do his part, and he came to me.

You're probably wondering why we still had contact with each other after the abuse stopped. It's really strange, but after I told my parents and they put a stop to the abuse, I wasn't the only one who buried it away in the depths of my mind: my parents did, too. While they made certain there was no more abuse, they continued to have a relationship with That Boy. We all acted as though it had never happened. In fact, a few years ago, I mentioned the abuse to my mother, and she said she didn't remember it. Ditto with Dad.

In talking with other people who've been sexually abused, I've discovered that this scenario isn't as unusual as it might seem. Apparently, sexual abuse is so horrific to contemplate that lots of people bury it in a deep, dark corner of their subconscious. I certainly can't blame my parents for "forgetting" because, Lord knows, that's precisely what I did for close to thirty years. Denial, as they say, isn't just a river in Egypt.

Anyway, when That Boy came to me for help I refused, not because of the past, but because what he asked me to do would have put unwarranted pressure on another person who was his most likely financial source. It wasn't as though that person actually owed him any money: **he** just felt he was owed in the way only the truly selfish can. So I told him I wouldn't do his dirty work.

That Boy was not a happy camper. So later, he called my home and left a disgusting, obscene message on my answering machine. It was so awful, so abusive, that every last detail of my childhood rushed to the forefront of my mind, along with all the emotions I had kept locked up for so long. I hated him for it all.

I screamed. I cried. I screamed some more. For two solid weeks I was a total emotional mess: at turns wild with fear and enraged enough to do him physical harm. And then I told myself it had to come to a stop. No more could he control me, abuse me, or affect the way I reacted to life.

It was time to confront That Boy.

Let me insert something very important here. Not everyone needs to—or should—confront someone who has hurt her deeply. I would never suggest confrontation if it might put someone in danger, either physically or psychologically. Nor do I think confrontation is necessary for everyone: we're all delightfully different, and must travel our own path to healing and fulfillment.

But confrontation was essential for me.

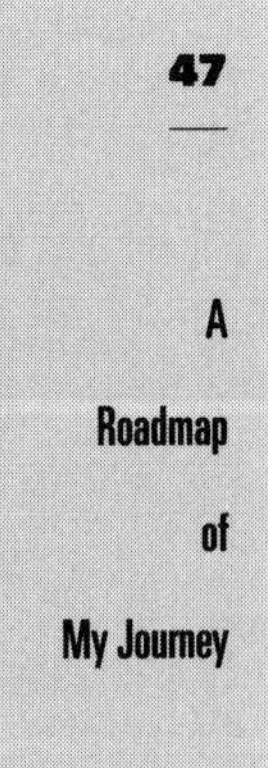

The first step I took was to write. I did that for twenty-one days. On the fourth day, I wrote That Boy and told him we had to talk, although I didn't say about what. I asked him to meet me at a restaurant that provided the safety of being public and the comfort of foods I love. That last bit might sound silly, but I knew I'd need everything I could lay my hands on to bolster me that day and a good piece of chocolate layer cake never hurt.

After I sent the letter, I continued to write. I titled my manuscript *21 Days of Happiness.* That may sound weird, considering why I was writing, but I knew, I just knew, that this writing and confronting That Boy were going to lead me into a dimension of happiness I'd never before experienced.

As I wrote, I tried to get back to the little girl I'd been to understand the woman I'd become. As I did that, I realized fully for the first time the role that exercise, eating right and dress had played in my life: they were all efforts to control my own body, all forms of armor to keep people from seeing the real me. No wonder I'd chosen to go into retail, clothing design and Jazzercise: they were simply professional extensions of controlling and hiding. Even my acts of service were a defense mechanism: if I concentrated on others, did things for them, it took the focus off me. No probing questions. No curiosity about my past.

I looked into my soul for three weeks. I'd put it off for nearly three decades, until I was capable, not only of looking inward, but also of handling what I found when I did. Don't get me wrong: handling it was difficult and it stretched me to the max, but it didn't break me completely the way it might have earlier in my life.

During those weeks, though, I was very emotional: I found that as I went back to find the little girl I'd been, I relived her fear, her insecurities, the terrible sense of being intimidated. Some people might consider that going backwards, but I knew that I could never really travel forward if I didn't come to terms with my past.

For three weeks I was fragile, lost, scared, vulnerable, and felt terribly ugly. I didn't feel like the attractive pillar of strength my friends and family believed me to be. And so I had to ask myself if the control I had over externals was truly strength. Was my physical attractiveness truly beauty?

I've told you that early in my life I recognized the power of externals. When I was little, I used to act out the role of a woman on an old Aqua Velva commercial. She was so beautiful and men loved her: she could control them with just a toss of her head. I got all kinds of attention when I imitated her. It was a standing joke in the family: "Come watch Joni do the Aqua Velva commercial." Even then I recognized the

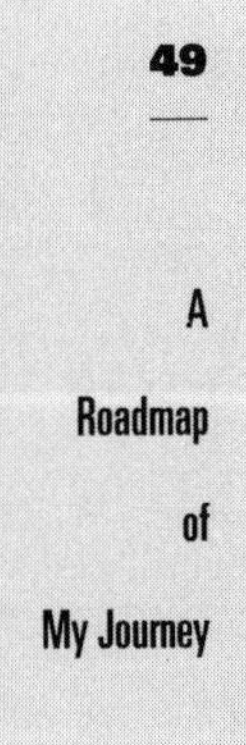

power of outer beauty, of externals, and I used it to function for the next thirty-some years. I was always busy, running from one thing to the next, involved in big things, the bigger the better, to earn attention and approval. No matter what time of day someone knocked on my door, I was dressed perfectly, hair in place, makeup on—simply dazzling.

But when the time came to truly come to terms with my past, I knew that the power of externals was not enough. I knew that externals might attract people, might make them like the me they could see, but what good was that if that wasn't really the me I was inside? What power did looking or doing good have to resolve the inner turmoil unleashed by that obscene phone message?

To find answers, I wrote and wrote and wrote for three weeks. I wrote about things of no particular consequence, or so it seemed then. I wrote about my hopes and wishes for my two dear daughters. I reveled in their healthy childhoods—so unlike mine—and my role as a mother in making them so.

Writing was a daily exercise in discipline and consistency and developing inner strength. It was the way I mustered the courage to drive to that restaurant and confront That Boy. I had to do it. I had to take control of my life, all of it—past, present and future—once and for all.

On the twenty-first day, I went to the restaurant where I'd asked him to meet me. I had no idea whether or not he'd show up. I was so nervous: my intuition told me he knew what was going to be discussed over the chicken salad. But I also knew that at last I was in control of the relationship.

He finally walked in the door. We made small talk. How weird! But he's been a part of my life for years, and we hadn't been together for a long time. Finally, I couldn't stand it anymore and I blurted it all out:

Why did you leave that disgusting message on my answering machine? Why did you hurt me over and over again when we were little? Why did you make me do those disgusting things? You screwed me up in so many ways: the way I think and feel and look at life is all messed up. I hate you, I hate you, *I hate you!*

I didn't cry. I was too angry. All those years, pent up, and finally **he** was the captive audience.

But all he could say was that he was sorry, so sorry. No answers to my repeated why's. It was strange, not like these scenes go in the movies. He was too quiet, sedate. I guess I'd expected him to fall apart and have answers to my questions on the tip of his tongue.

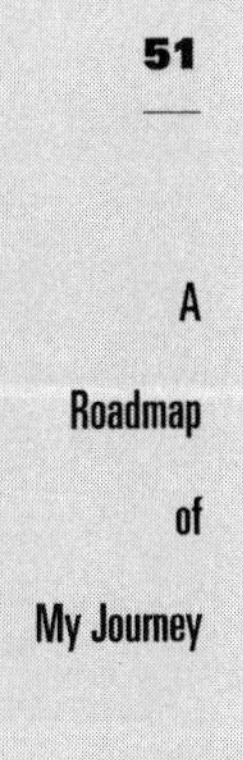

When I was finally talked out, we ate, went back to small talk, then got up and walked away from each other. I haven't seen him since.

I went home and I wrote. I wasn't immediately aware of what that confrontation had given me, but I soon realized that it set in motion a period of intense self-examination that jump-started my continuing journey to true happiness.

Externals could take me only so far, give me only outer beauty, a form of strength and happiness. Confronting That Boy gave me the courage to look inside and focus on developing inner beauty. I considered many, many aspects of being a woman as I began that leg of the journey and came to terms with my past.

I thought about why we make excuses. How to focus on our dreams and the role that discipline, courage, and serving others play in making them come true. I considered what it means to be a lady and how sensuality and mystery relate to that. I examined the impact that perfect strangers and perfect friends have on our lives. The importance of prayer and my relationship with God.

Each of the following chapters deals with one of these aspects. Towards the end of the book, I've also written about those externals that kept me going for so long. There are some of us who need to start with what's on the outside: if

I'd tried to deal with what was inside me earlier in my life, it would have destroyed me. And even if you're starting your journey to happiness on the inside, it helps to get a healthy perspective on exercise, dress and nutrition. Some of you may even consider coming to terms with those externals your biggest challenge.

We're all different, and while we share a mutual destination—happiness—our individual journeys to reach it may follow very different paths. But one thing is true for all of us:

> A journey of a thousand miles
> must begin with a single step.
>
> LAO-TSU, *c.* 604 – *c.* 531 B.C.

EXCUSES:

BARRIERS TO GROWTH

IF WE'RE GOING TO GROW, we must stop making excuses for why things are not happening the way we'd like them to, for why we're not happy. I mentioned this in an earlier chapter, but because it's so important, I want to elaborate on it here.

Remember: we set the stage for our own magic carpet ride. When we're on that stage, we're the performers, and we control the audience. If something isn't working to our advantage, then we should change it, play with it, be flexible and make it work for us. We have the freedom to change the backdrop on our stage as often as we wish. It takes mega-doses of commitment and discipline, but it can be accomplished.

No more explanations and excuses. No one wants to hear them anyway.

Everyone has bad things happen to them: that's life. If you've read the previous chapter, you know that something terrible happened to me in childhood. I can't change what happened, so I have just two options: to let it control me for the rest of my life, or to control it.

Let me make one thing clear here. *Control* does not mean erase it completely. I can deal with my past, come to terms with it, so to speak, but I do recognize that it will influence me throughout my life: I still have horrible reactions to situations that trigger memories of that time. What I can control, however, is the extent of that influence by the degree to which I react.

There is no such thing as a charmed life. When we see someone who appears to be living one, if we look closer what we'll really see is someone who is working her buns off to set her own stage, adjust her attitude over and over again, and make life work for her. She may not be able to keep life from handing her lemons, but she's developed some nifty recipes for lemonade.

A woman like that makes handling difficulties look easy, usually because she's made hard work a way of life, and plays just as hard. Hard work looks easy on others when they have made a good habit of it and enjoy what they do.

Enjoying what we do makes for a magical existence. Let's say no to the things we don't care for: and no excuses here, either. A simple "no, thank you" does the job. Feel the freedom of it all. It is exhilarating, and the healthiest thing we can do for ourselves.

We cut way down on excuses if we enjoy what we do and whom we choose to spend time with. There are times, of course, when we have responsibilities we may not enjoy, but even then we can choose to adjust our attitude to get all the enjoyment we can from the situation.

Making excuses relays to others that we don't have control of our lives, that we have to blame something or someone other than ourselves. When we find ourselves making excuses, it's time to take the responsibility of working hard to control our lives.

During those dreadful years of my childhood, I believed myself to be quite the ugly duckling because That Boy told me repeatedly that I was. It took years before I felt beautiful, but by the ripe old age of thirty-three I guess I was feeling pretty sure of myself, at least on the outside, and I entered the Mrs. Ohio pageant. Whatever possessed me, I'll never know: I'd never done anything like it before in my life.

But something inside me pushed me to enter, so I did.

Getting ready for the Mrs. Ohio pageant was quite a task: clothes to buy—and you know how perfect they had to be—written evaluations to be filled out, and an attitude that had to be honed. It was a busy and nerve-racking couple of months, but I was filled with excitement.

The pageant was being held 250 miles from home, and I had absolutely no idea what I was going to encounter when I got there. In the back of my mind, though, I truly believed that the judges would be looking for an older, mature, interesting woman who was the wiser for being happily married.

As the weekend progressed, I realized that I had been sadly mistaken. They were looking for an older version of Miss America, complete with sequins and T&A. Besides that, most of the contestants had been in pageants for years, and knew all the ropes. (Shoot, I didn't even know how to turn at the end of the runway.) And on top of that, the atmosphere of female cattiness was enough to suffocate the strongest woman.

So there I was: four hours from home, alone, and in a situation I no longer wanted to be in.

Did I let that situation control me? Did I quit? Question my own values and try to shape myself into what the judges were looking for? Get depressed because I wasn't pretty enough or had the wrong clothes? Did I let those catty women get to me? Did I feel sorry for myself and make excuses?

Absolutely not!

I took that "lemon" and I made lemonade. I kept my mouth shut and eyes and ears open and learned all I could that weekend. I put on my armor against the cattiness, and used my strength to help protect some of the sweeter, softer women, who, like me, were just winging the whole experience.

It was a real lesson in strength covering insecurity—and it worked.

I think the judges were, in fact, looking for a married floozy. But I stayed true to myself and my values—which do not include being a married floozy—and I ended up as one of ten finalists. I kept the plaque, not because I'm proud that I was a finalist, but as a reminder that I worked my tail off for it. I even purchased a videotape of the pageant, although it took two years before I had the courage to watch it—alone, in my dark basement, in the middle of the night.

And do you know what I learned when I did? That I was smart! That when I smile, I dazzle people! Watching that tape was exactly the experience I needed to move forward at that point in my journey, to believe more than ever in myself and the direction I was taking in life. It was the first successful assault on my ugly-duckism and feeling like a seven-year-old flunky who had to repeat second grade.

I mentioned that when I entered Mrs. Ohio, I didn't know exactly why. Life is like that sometimes. We do things, not knowing the reason. We're simply compelled. Then, much later, we understand.

That is why it is essential to try, to stretch and follow through. What we gain is a greater understanding of ourselves and the world around us.

I didn't become Mrs. Ohio like I once hoped. I undertook that journey with the highest expectations, but they were focused in the wrong direction. I learned much more by losing than by winning, and I held onto life's most important crown, self-respect.

And I would have gained none of that if I'd made excuses.

What we call luck is
opportunity meeting readiness.
So let's be better prepared than the average Susie
when opportunity knocks.
Prepared with everything but excuses.

FOCUSING ON OUR

FOCUSING ON OUR

What we call luck is
opportunity meeting readiness.
So let's be better prepared than the average Susie
when opportunity knocks.
Prepared with everything but excuses.

DREAMS

Dreams are necessary to life.

ANAÏS NIN

AS YOU TAKE YOUR MAGIC CARPET RIDE, I want you to feel and dig and unlock and soar.

I want you to really look at your attributes, not your negatives. Concentrate on what is positive in your life and build on it to change what needs to be changed in order to be your best. That's the only way you can maximize your potential, fulfill your dreams, and become kind, strong, giving and powerful.

Those positives *are* there; I guarantee it!

If you've been through one of life's rough spots and lived to talk about it, you've automatically developed positive qualities. Simply by virtue of being a woman, you have a number of positive characteristics and abilities—remember *muliebrity?*—that you can use to shape your future.

Self-examination is an emotional ride, I know, but that's part of taking a good, hard look at ourselves.

I think we know intuitively when the time is right for self-examination, and I also believe we don't necessarily do it all at once. Nor should we force those times. But when they come, each a stage in our journey to happiness, we shouldn't procrastinate. That won't make the issues deep down inside go away: like a diver who needs to resurface for air, they'll come rushing to the surface and break through the seeming calm of our lives when we least expect them.

When each period of self-examination is over, we'll have found another best part of ourselves. And then—and only then—can we make that work for us and share it so it works for everyone we touch.

I know that's what can happen, because I've done it by writing this book.

A dream is a wish your heart makes.

FROM WALT DISNEY'S *Cinderella*

What are your dreams? And don't tell me you don't have them. Every woman has hopes in life that won't be denied: they drive us.

So, I ask you again: what are your dreams? What is it that you want to do? To become? What dreams do you grant yourself? Are they big, or small, secret, but equally worthy dreams you long to pursue?

But now that I've asked, don't tell me. Your dreams should be your secret, never to be divulged. As women, we have the strength of mystery, and we should hold on to that incredible asset. Just work quietly towards making your dreams come true, and let the rest of the world marvel at your accomplishments.

Our dreams come in all sizes, shapes and colors: the life and choices they represent are our very own. Always remember that what's good for one person may not be good for another. Your mother's or sister's or husband's or friend's dreams may not be the same as yours, and rarely is life spent more miserably than when we try to pursue a dream that is not truly ours.

That doesn't mean that we shouldn't look for what's good in others lives—kindness, gentleness, warmth, determination—and learn how to develop those qualities in our own. Which brings me to another point.

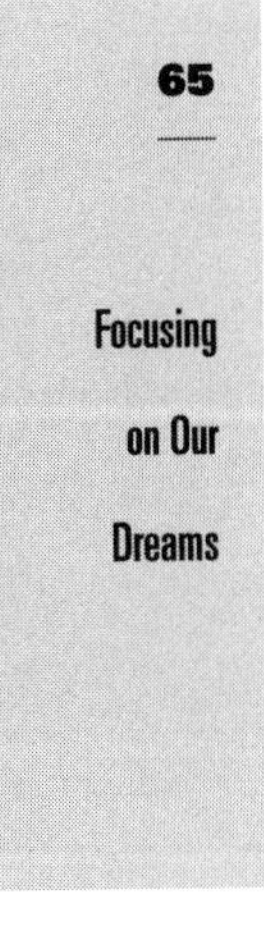

I see an alarming tendency today to pattern our lifestyles after the so-called rich and famous. Of course, some celebrities do have admirable qualities. But do they really have the most to teach us? If we think back, won't we discover that most of the individuals who made a significant difference in our lives were very ordinary folks like us who were full of love?

We should not always look to an athlete or politician or supermodel or movie star for inspiration. Instead, we should draw inspiration from people in our own backyards who have been transformed from ordinary to extraordinary through their expression of love for others.

One of the chief enemies of maximizing our potential is busyness. I'm talking here, not about living a full life, but about being busy for busy's sake. Too many people today run around like chickens with their heads cut off and fail to truly enjoy the quality of life, the sweetness of it all.

Please, let's stop always saying how busy we are: no one really cares. Instead, let's ask ourselves *why* we're always busy.

Are we trying to impress people? Well, we won't, and even trying may indicate a rather ugly need to exalt ourselves at others' expense. Even if we're not trying to impress, but simply use busyness as an excuse, aren't we revealing the horrible fact that activities take priority over people in our lives?

Trying to impress ourselves? Being busy for busy's sake—rather than for the sake of something we really love—is, ultimately, an ineffective method of building self-esteem. We only build confidence by achieving things we value.

Do we keep ourselves busy in order to avoid facing life's important issues, such as working towards our dreams, filling our time instead with less meaningful activity that creates the illusion of a life well lived? At the end of our life, which do you think we'll value more: a fulfilled life or a life filled with doing for doing's sake, or, in my case, for the sake of keeping the past blocked out of my consciousness?

I've been there: more and more projects, and the bigger, the better. I kept busy because I was too scared to take a good look inside myself and face the reality of my past. If you've been there, you know what I mean: life is good, things are running in order, but there is that great big unnamed emptiness inside because we know in our heart and soul that we will have to eventually look our problem smack in the eye, and we are so darned scared at the prospect. But face it: when the time is right we must if we are to be free to pursue our dreams and be happy.

The most important part of fulfilling dreams may not be the dreams themselves. Maybe we want to be better mothers, or become physically fit, or be able to entertain groups of people without being nervous, or change jobs.

What's most important, most lasting, most fulfilling is not necessarily the end result, but rather the inner qualities we develop in the process of achieving our dreams. Once we have those inner qualities, no one can take them away from us, and we can build on them throughout our lives to do even greater things. I'm sure you already have some of them: these are those positives I spoke of earlier. Building on those is integral to personal fulfillment and happiness.

This above all: to thine own self be true,
And it must follow, as the night the day,
Thou canst not then be false to any man.

WILLIAM SHAKESPEARE

I've said that your dreams are yours alone. But what if your vision for life is so far from the mainstream that you feel like a misfit? What if you find that you are a misfit in other areas of life?

First, I imagine that every single one of you reading this book has felt that way at one time. But being a misfit can be an asset if we decide to view it that way.

Misfits are true individuals. And I believe that, in that sense, being a misfit is a good thing. Isn't it incredible when we get attention because of what's unique about us?

Part of the problem is the word itself: *misfit.* It implies that something's wrong with us—when absolutely nothing is. We're mavericks: independent, self-styled. We're part of a tradition of great thinkers, inventors and pioneers who refused to be stopped by those dirty words, "It's never been done that way before." We put our stamp on the world, not the other way around. And in all, we are fueled by our muliebrity: we are kind, strong, giving and powerful.

Put that way, isn't being a misfit delectable?

For me, being a misfit has been a way of life. I never thought I fit the mold or what I thought the mold was supposed to be, because that meant being a follower. And in my childhood, following—doing what That Boy told me, forced me, to do—brought only ugliness and hurt. Once the abuse ended, I cut myself off totally from anyone who told me how I should be. I've never been able to bring myself to do things the way they're supposed to be done, not exactly, anyway. I feel compelled to give things my special touch, nudge them just a bit left of center. Be the odd woman out, the square peg in a round hole.

Voilà! I'm a misfit. And I'm not complaining, because it actually makes me happier.

But what comes with this territory is loneliness, at least at times. People don't view the world the way we do. Nor do they choose the same pieces we would to put life's puzzles together. As a result, we misfits often work alone. It's easier: no explaining to be done. Yes, there are sometimes people along the way, as resilient and flexible as we are, with whom we work superbly because we respect one another's individuality. But most of the time, we misfits travel our road solo.

But loneliness—maybe it's more accurate to call the misfit's loneliness *aloneness*—can be healthy if we approach it with a positive attitude. It gives us the time we need to examine ourselves and work toward our dreams. We gain incredible strength during periods of aloneness by leaning more than ever on our faith and values. And every little twist we put on life takes us one step closer to complete happiness.

If you think you're a misfit, you're not alone. Every woman I know thinks there are ways in which she doesn't fit in. And that includes women who are beautiful, popular, successful—the last females on earth you'd consider misfits. That's why it's important to support one another as we pursue our dreams, different as they may be.

As you pursue yours, let's remember those wonderful individuals who helped us along the way. The ones who made us so incredibly different, delectable misfits. We can pay them no greater compliment than to let them know that their words of love and encouragement, their example, helped make us kind, strong, giving, and powerful.

Speaking of others, let me say a few words here about the way others view us. It's important to keep our perspective on this, or we can get off course.

Personally, I've discovered that most people, unless they know us very, very well, see only one dimension of our personality.

In my case, men and women seem to perceive me as some sort of sex kitten. Let me give you an example.

I was in a Jazzercise class the other day: I know the instructor quite well, since we've worked together for about thirteen years.

The instructor mentioned that she'd seen the new James Bond movie, and the leading lady was very sexy. Then, in front of the entire class, she said, "Oh, Joni, you would love her: she is just like you, dark hair, red lips, *etc., etc.*"

Some people might have considered that a compliment, but I was embarrassed. What about all my other attributes? What about the fact that I am kind and smart and have a happy family? Why do some people fail to embrace the "wholeness" of us?

That I can't answer: maybe they don't know us very well, or maybe it's a human tendency to label and categorize others. But we have to be prepared for that to happen.

The truth is, I probably am sexy (although I prefer to think of myself as sensual: more about that in a later chapter). What bothers me is that sexiness is the only thing some people see. There's probably a bit of a negative reaction because of my childhood, too. However, I can't change the way others perceive me, and I shouldn't try, unless it's my goal to change some undesirable quality they're picking up on. The one thing I absolutely must not do is let their reaction knock me off the path to my dreams.

Bottom line, ladies, it all comes down to having confidence in yourself.

So remember that your journey to personal fulfillment and happiness won't take place overnight: it may take years. Don't sell yourself short by giving up, no matter how long it takes, no matter how others treat you along the way. Be traditional when it makes sense or it's absolutely required.

But those other times, give life your own twist: be a maverick. And above all, truly believe, with all your heart and soul, that your dreams can come true.

In the long run men hit only what they aim at.

HENRY DAVID THOREAU

DISCIPLINE:

YOUR BEST FRIEND

OKAY. YOU'VE JUST READ THE TITLE of this chapter, and you're thinking to yourself, "I was with her right up until now. But I can't take one more person telling me that if I just got up a little earlier, did a little more, tried a little harder, I could have it all."

Good! I'm glad if that's what you think. Because I'm not talking about that SuperWoman-you-can-have-it-all-including-a-nervous-breakdown rubbish too many of us bought in the Seventies and Eighties. When I say *discipline*, I'm not talking about doing more or working harder.

By discipline, I mean doing more of what gets us to our dreams, less of what doesn't. Working smarter, not harder. Moderation, if you will.

Did you know that *moderation* is a synonym for discipline? Unfortunately, it's not a synonym that got much press during the last two decades.

But there are signs that we're realizing the futility of our obsessive society: even Jane "Go-for-the-burn" Fonda says she went overboard on exercise, and now does *moderate* workouts. Have you seen her picture lately? She looks terrific, and, more important, she looks happy.

Discipline is a full word. Let's look at its many meanings: *a set of rules or methods; training expected to produce a specific pattern of behavior; controlled behavior; a branch of knowledge; punishment intended to correct or change; moderation.*

A set of rules or methods. We're not talking about long lists of picky do's and don'ts. Discipline in the sense I mean it is very positive.

For example, one of our rules, or disciplines, should be never to abandon our values. When we've discovered what our values are, we should hang on tight to them because they will carry us through every single area of our life.

Another rule should be to use our senses, the strongest of which is intuition. Yet another, to spend time with people who share our values and have a zest for living that keeps them moving forward and upward.

We've too often equated discipline with lists and schedules. Most of us are terribly guilty of this mania. Let's stop making lists and use that time to lie back and enjoy. It's funny: those lists are supposed to help, but all they end up doing is putting more pressure on us. If there are no lists, then we simply do what is important, our priorities. (Don't throw away your calendar, however: you need it for appointments, and there's nothing worse than forgetting one.)

What about methods? Well, we're all individuals. Even if our dreams were identical, chances are we'd get to them in different ways: our journey to happiness and fulfillment is ours alone. But there are some things that helped me, some elements of life and muliebrity that I considered, and you're learning about them as you read this book. You might call some of them methods.

Training expected to produce a specific pattern of behavior. This is so important, because the wrong training can result in behavior that makes us so unhappy.

For example, in my early years, I was trained. Ah, yes. I was trained to respond to That Boy. It didn't matter what I was involved in: when he was ready for me, I had to go and behave the way he taught me. Expected, forced behavior no one was ever to be told about. I did what he said—quietly, miserably, unhappily.

Fortunately, as an older child and adult, I discovered that the training I needed was far different than that forced upon me for so many years. Discipline in this sense of the word is actually learning how to zero in and target the situations in life that truly make us happy and help us move closer to our wants and desires: *training expected to produce a specific*—good for us—*pattern of behavior.*

Through trial and error I discovered that one of my "wants" was getting positive attention, and so I trained myself to do good things in order to get it. Those "good things" done openly were so different than the sneaky things being done to me behind closed doors and bushes and trees.

Controlled behavior? For many of us, it's learning to say "no." It's always okay to say "no." Anytime. Anywhere. It's our prerogative. I know that now, better than most.

I love the exhilaration of saying that simple syllable that puts me in charge.

"No" comes in handy if our schedule is so full that we're walking through life unsmiling and selfish, riding on that dreadful, whiny, complaining wagon. That's when we need to control our behavior by learning to say "no"—preferably "no, thank you," with a smile.

Let me explain something here. Most of us can handle tons of stuff— after all, we're women—as long as we feel it's contributing to making our dreams come true. Think about it. When you're doing something you truly enjoy, can't you stick with it for hours and not tire? Most of us also realize that there are some things in life, like cleaning toilets, that we may not be crazy about doing, but that have to be done, and we can adjust to that.

It's the truly non-essential stuff that isn't getting us to our dreams that turns us into whining complainers. We've lost our balance, our equilibrium: the non-essentials have become too weighty, and they're throwing our entire life off kilter: we're doing too much that drains us, and not enough that enriches us. And we react to that unbalanced state by whining.

So from now on, when we hear ourselves use that awful tone of voice, or realize that people who count aren't paying attention to what we're saying anymore, let's make a pact to "control" our behavior and stop whining. Then we should take a look at our lives, see where we're getting weighed down, and decide what needs to be rearranged or has to go.

So discipline can help us contend with our busy schedules, because it helps us focus on what's important, and teaches us when to push and when to pull back on what we're doing. It helps us maintain our balance.

A branch of knowledge. What are we going to know about? Ourselves, my friends. By the time we complete our journey to happiness, we should know ourselves better than anyone else on earth.

Now that may sound silly to some of you, but lots of people don't know who they are, what they want, where they're going. And we simply can't get anywhere that way. I love this quote, although I'm not sure who first said it:

**You are the only person
with whom
you will share every moment of your life.**

Good enough reason to know yourself through-and-through, I think.

Punishment intended to correct or change. No beating ourselves up here, okay? It's counterproductive to get down on ourselves because we're not making progress. So let's concentrate instead on that phrase "correct or change."

Next time we fail to say "no" when we should, and we end up feeling lousy, we won't let ourselves focus on that feeling (which is the "punishment" part). Instead, let's focus on what we could have done differently. Why didn't we turn that person down? How could we do it gracefully next time? We must have the discipline to change our behavior, rather than indulge in self-pity.

Moderation. How I love that word! It's not all or nothing. Don't believe that. Let's adopt a new motto: "It's moderation *and* everything!"

Deprivation is negative. Rigid schedules stifle us. So let's keep a little bit of everything we love in our lives. Let's do something on the spur of the moment: it's rejuvenating to be off your schedule for a while. When we mix it all up, it's fun and goofy and we get a fresh outlook on the everyday things of life.

And now, a final thought on discipline.

Discipline comes from the Latin word, *disciplina.* The word *disciple* comes from that same word. A disciple is one who embraces and assists in spreading the teachings of another. Heavy stuff. We need to take a good look at this.

Remember that our goal is to become kind, strong, giving, and powerful. Keep in mind, too, that good disciples usually end up teaching others what they learn (think about great religious figures like Jesus, Mohammed, Baha'u'llah and Buddha: their disciples were responsible for spreading their teachings).

If we're giving, aren't we, too, going to share what we learn in life? Aren't we going to become strong and powerful teachers? And if we're kind, aren't we going to share what we know in a way that always helps, never hurts? That is a heavy responsibility. But we women can be the greatest teachers.

In a completely rational society, the best of us would aspire to be teachers and the rest would settle for something less, because passing civilization along from one generation to the next ought to be the highest responsibility anyone could have.

LEE IACOCCA

Every single one of us has something special to share with others, something that can make a difference.

Oh, sure, there are people out there who may have made us feel worthless. But you know what?

They're full of hogwash!

Right now, today, this very minute, you've got something that could help someone else. So don't be afraid to reach out and share it with those around you, especially the joy and the freedom you're gaining as you employ every aspect of discipline to pursue your dreams.

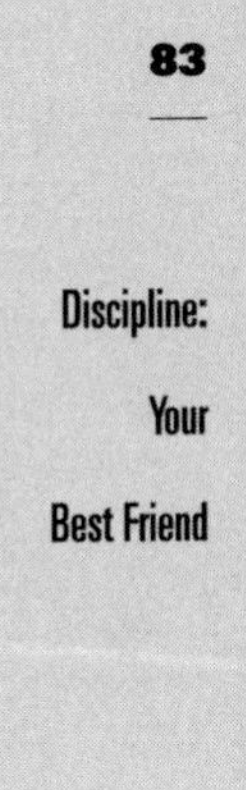

THE COURAGE TO THE

CHANGE. COURAGE TO SERVE.

Change is but one side of a coin.
Courage is the other.

CHANGE IS THE ONE CONSTANT IN LIFE: we may try to control it, but like it or not, we are joined to it at the hip. So we must learn to accept change, even try with all our might to encourage it. Because with it comes the magic carpet ride out of many a hellhole and into the gates of a heavenly existence.

We can fight change. We can drown in it. Or we can welcome it. Use it to grow, to help others, to become the happy women we all want to be. But accepting change, using it to shape the direction of our own course and that of the world takes a mammoth amount of courage, because for many of us, change is scary.

What is courage? I think it's the quality of being bold. A sense of fearlessness. Standing up in the face of adversity. And I also believe that in a society that has elevated self-concern to an art form, one of the greatest acts of courage a woman can perform is to purposely serve others.

Writing this book has taken great courage. Let's face it: right now, I feel as though my life is as transparent as Saran Wrap. But what good is my complete happiness, gained by coming to terms with my past, if I don't share how I attained it? I wrote this book to serve us all.

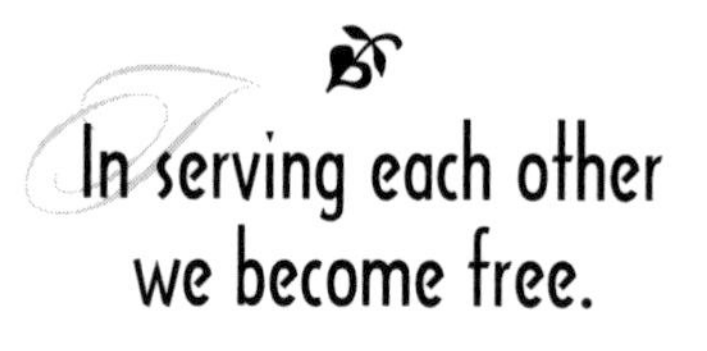

—MOTTO OF KING ARTHUR'S CAMELOT,
FROM THE FILM, *First Knight*

The benefits of serving others are endless. Something as simple as bringing a smile to another's lips is an incredible gift of service, and as easy as turning up the corners of our mouth first. But because we fear rejection, smiling first takes that thing called courage.

What if she doesn't smile back? Well, hang on, because the truth is that she usually doesn't, at least not immediately.

Ah, but if we can hang on to that smile and summon up our courage to maintain eye contact for another ten seconds—*voilà*—we will encounter the most beautiful sight, another's smile. And we will also have—if just for a second—changed our world for the better.

I have been on both sides of this scenario. Remember: I was the girl who found it difficult to smile. So when I was little and someone took time to get me to smile, it felt so good, and the look on that person's face just made it feel better. There we were: two warm beacons of light, illuminating that particular space and time for a single, perfect, shared moment.

After a while, I found that sharing smiles was so simple, yet it made me so happy. No words, no touch, just brilliant smiles that helped heal me. As a result, by the time my childhood had passed, my smile was a permanent fixture on my face.

Let's always remember the beauty, the power, of a simple smile. When we smile, we make another human being feel important, special, even loved, for a single moment in time. And in some lives, unfortunately, that single moment may be the only speck of caring that person has experienced in ages.

We also do something for ourselves with that smile. We exercise our courage. We gain freedom from that moment because we're in charge, reaching out first in the face of potential rejection. We sucked in a deep breath, stepped outside of our comfort zone, and *willingly served.*

In turn, we realized an exhilarating freedom that can become habitual, intoxicating to us, and contagious to others. And that, my darlings, is what it's all about: that's when we start to change the world—and ourselves—for the better.

It is gently raining.
Yet, we see the rainbow.

As women, we see much in our world that needs to be changed, many areas that cry out for our service. For me, it began down by the river with my small, injured animals. I was learning, serving in my own little way, although I was unaware at the time that I was. All I knew was that it made me feel good, gave me a kind of strength to carry on: my very first lesson in the experience of being healed in my unselfish desire to serve others.

In our heart of hearts, we know when things are not the way they should be, that circumstances exist that no one should have to live with. We sense there should be a change, even a mutiny—and you know what? We should lead it!

We, as women, are the ones who can. Women are survivors, pure and simple. And over the centuries, while men were busy getting their names in the history books, we were the ones quietly shaping the day-to-day life that is the very foundation of civilization.

That took courage then, and it takes courage now. But in the end, the world is better for our courage, and so are we.

Courage and change go hand-in-hand:
The wings on which we soar, expand.

IN OUR

WRITE MINDS

YOUR MIND IS A GREAT TREASURE: within it, you can say and think whatever you want, and nobody knows what's going on in there unless you choose to tell them. I love that!

I mean, you're out there in public, and you're visible, but people really haven't got a clue about what is going on in that beautiful mind of yours. And that's good, because a lot of what matters to us most is very private, too precious, too fragile, too hurtful to share with even the closest friend.

That's one reason I like to write. Writing gives me a chance to say privately exactly what's in my heart and on my mind. No holds barred.

Writing out what I'm thinking helps me understand what's troubling me, what issues of my life need to be addressed. As I mentioned earlier, this book grew out of a time four years ago when I wrote for three weeks in order to get up the courage to confront That Boy about the sexual abuse he had inflicted on me when I was little.

The words I put on paper during those three weeks gave me substance and courage and impetus: I couldn't have confronted him without having written about how I felt. And if I had never confronted him, I'd have never known the happiness I do today.

(Please remember, as I cautioned earlier, that confrontation isn't for everyone. If there's even the slightest chance it will put you in physical danger, or it's more than you can handle emotionally, *don't do it.* We all have our own paths to happiness, and confrontation may not need to be a stop along the way on yours.)

Writing has always been a way for me to "get it all out," even in less critical circumstances. I'll bet it's the same for many of you: didn't you keep a diary at some time in your life? I encourage you to start again!

Am I a writer? That's tough for me to answer. No, I have not been formally trained to write, except for a few creative writing courses here and there. Those, I truly enjoyed.

Yet writing is in my bones. My dad is a fantastic writer and so are my six siblings.

When I think hard, I can go back to my first attempts at writing. You know how in grade school we all used to write little notes back and forth in arithmetic class? How I hated arithmetic. But passing notes, that was a different story.

Because of those notes, I discovered at an early age the power of written communication: that's another reason I like to write. It was incredible to me that I could write down a few kind words to another person and create an immeasurable amount of happiness for them as well as for myself. It was a great learning experience, and I carry it with me to this day.

That's why I kick myself when I forget to—or, I should say, get sidetracked from—writing a thank-you note. It means the world to me when I receive one, so I figure it means that much to someone else to get one, too. Some consider thank-you notes old-fashioned. To me, they're a beautiful way of capturing your appreciation for someone's kindness and time.

Over the years, I've also discovered that when I'm not able to make people understand what I'm saying verbally, I can usually communicate my thoughts to them if I put them on paper. Words on paper allow the reader to read and re-read with no interruptions. And it's easier for some people to focus their eyes than their ears.

In our highly-visual, fast-paced world of mass communication, writing doesn't seem as important to some people as it once was. Let's not be those people. Let's use postcards, e-mail, faxes, notes scribbled on the backs of grocery lists if we must: but somehow, someway, let's make every effort to communicate in writing with friends and family. Conversations, as special as they may be, cannot be pressed between the pages of a scrapbook, their love and wisdom and laughter preserved to be savored over and over again.

Writing is an invaluable tool in serving others. I've already mentioned thank-you notes. Then there are condolence notes. No, not when-you-care-enough-to-send-the-very-best-pre-printed sympathy cards we simply sign, but the kind where we start with a blank page and express our love and empathy in a very personal way that says we care even more.

Remember when someone took the time to write you a letter or a nice long note in a card? There are few better gifts you can receive. In fact, when you get your mail, don't you open the handwritten notes first? Of course you do! So break out pen and paper and let's make someone's day better.

re-read with no interruptions. And it's easier for some people to focus their eyes than their ears.

In our highly-visual, fast-paced world of mass communication, writing doesn't seem as important to some people as it once was. Let's not be those people. Let's use postcards, e-mail, faxes, notes scribbled on the backs of grocery lists if we must: but somehow, someway, let's make every effort to communicate in writing with friends and family. Conversations, as special as they may be, cannot be pressed between the pages of a scrapbook, their love and wisdom and laughter preserved to be savored over and over again.

Writing is an invaluable tool in serving others. I've already mentioned thank-you notes. Then there are condolence notes. No, not when-you-care-enough-to-send-the-very-best-pre-printed sympathy cards we simply sign, but the kind where we start with a blank page and express our love and empathy in a very personal way that says we care even more.

Remember when someone took the time to write you a letter or a nice long note in a card? There are few better gifts you can receive. In fact, when you get your mail, don't you open the handwritten notes first? Of course you do! So break out pen and paper and let's make someone's day better.

Yet writing is in my bones. My dad is a fantastic writer and so are my six siblings.

When I think hard, I can go back to my first attempts at writing. You know how in grade school we all used to write little notes back and forth in arithmetic class? How I hated arithmetic. But passing notes, that was a different story.

Because of those notes, I discovered at an early age the power of written communication: that's another reason I like to write. It was incredible to me that I could write down a few kind words to another person and create an immeasurable amount of happiness for them as well as for myself. It was a great learning experience, and I carry it with me to this day.

That's why I kick myself when I forget to—or, I should say, get sidetracked from—writing a thank-you note. It means the world to me when I receive one, so I figure it means that much to someone else to get one, too. Some consider thank-you notes old-fashioned. To me, they're a beautiful way of capturing your appreciation for someone's kindness and time.

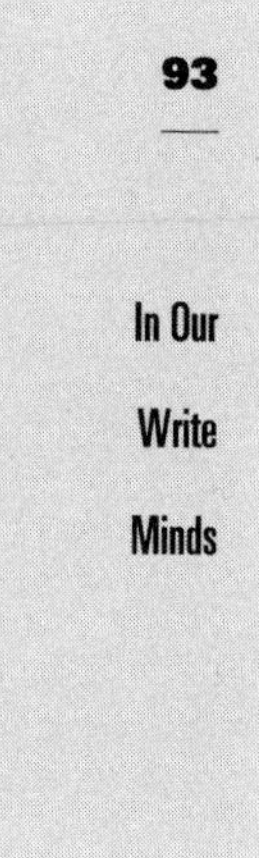

Over the years, I've also discovered that when I'm not able to make people understand what I'm saying verbally, I can usually communicate my thoughts to them if I put them on paper. Words on paper allow the reader to read and

Several years ago, I started to write long letters to my children on their birthdays. I told them of my love for them, my hopes, my prayers. My children know nothing of these letters. I am saving each and every one for them, and I'm confident that I'll know the perfect time to give each of my beautiful daughters her whole loving bundle.

Long after the presents are forgotten, long after the memories of parties are faded, and, yes, long after I am gone, those letters will continue to serve my children, bolstering them with the knowledge of how much they were cherished at each stage of their lives.

I believe that writing reinforces those qualities we seek to attain as women. When we write for ourselves we become stronger and more powerful. When we write for others, we grow increasingly kind and giving.

So, dear friends, let us never pass up an opportunity to liberate ourselves and serve others through the written word.

ON BEING

A LADY

Step aside, fellas: we're coming through!

BEING A LADY IS ONE OF OUR GRANDEST ASSETS. We need to use this marvelous "positive" to our advantage.

Don't let anyone mislead you. Chivalry is not dead: a man *wants* to feel like a gentleman. A *gentleman* is just that, a gentle man. *Lady* is the gentle side of femininity. And like appeals to like: when we're gentle women , *i.e.* ladies, we inspire men to be gentlemen.

It takes a bit of time to be gentle. It means we have to slow down occasionally so that we can find the softer side of ourselves.

Being a lady does not mean losing power or strength. On the contrary, when we use the softer side of our femininity, we gain immeasurable amounts of control. I'm not talking here about the cutesy-pie-oh-you're-such-a-big-strong-man-and-little-ol'-me-is-just-so-lucky-to-be-your-doormat-and/or but-what-I'm-really-doing-is-manipulating-you-like-heck brand of control associated with faux femininity. I'm talking about true control that results from the kind of feminine strength and dignity I learned from my own mother, and I also see and admire in Margaret Thatcher, former prime minister of Great Britain.

My mom is a "lady's lady." She had seven children—boom, boom, bing, bing. There are only thirteen years between the oldest and youngest: you can imagine the potential for chaos when we were little. Mom sailed through it all, serene and beautiful.

Later on as we grew older, Mom had to cope with family members who abused drugs and alcohol, and/or were mentally ill. Despite these problems, she was proud of her family, and she wore her quiet dignity like a suit of armor. To this day, I stand amazed at her ability to smile and look as though life was rolling along smoothly when it was anything but.

Some might say Mom's smile was denial. But I think that she was trying to find a ray of sunshine in circumstances that threatened to envelope her in darkness. *Smile and the world smiles with you.* And God knows, Mom needed the world's smiles.

Throughout all her troubles, Mom's manners and etiquette remained impeccable. That's how she stayed true to herself. She was thoughtful to her husband, her children, and her friends, remembering those little details that sometimes seem trivial to all but the individual who cares about them deeply. Mom also managed to look great, pulled together when chaos reigned around her. And always, always, always, she kept her little red lipstick close at hand.

I learned a lot from Mom, but one thing in particular sticks: Mom knew that beauty is one of the most powerful components of femininity. Mom knew beauty is confidence.

I'm not talking here about the beauty our society associates with supermodels and movie stars. No, indeed. I'm talking about that unique part of each of us that radiates from the inside out to make each of us beautiful in our own special way. We all have it, but unless we recognize it ourselves, it's rare that others do.

My mother was not beautiful in the oodles-of-lace mode. Hers was the beauty that came from the confidence to find the best part of herself and hang onto it when people she loved dearly were so very, very troubled.

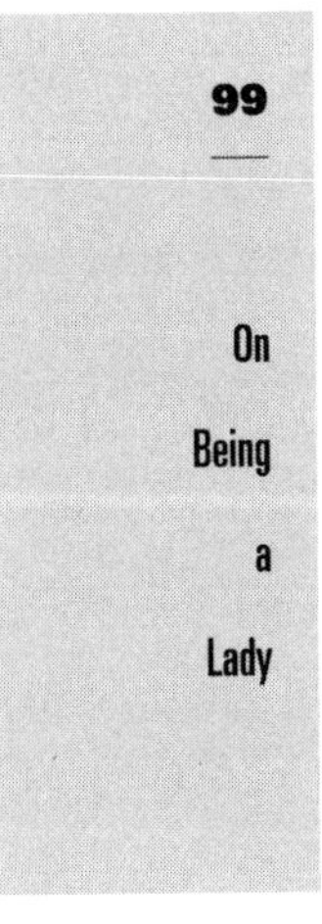

Margaret Thatcher is like my mom: strong, confident, and obviously a lady in her carriage, her walk, and her talk. Her dress is completely feminine. In all that she is and all she accomplishes, she consistently makes a statement: I am proud to be a woman. If you want a textbook on being a lady (since my mother doesn't have a book out) read Margaret Thatcher's autobiography.

Remember the late 1970s, when it was quite fashionable to dress like a man in business? Women felt it might give them an edge, a leg up.

Never!

Have we ever asked the male population its feelings on this subject? If we took a poll, men would tell us how much they hated it. How would we feel if men seriously started dressing like women? We'd think, "What are you, nuts?" We want men to be gentlemen, and men want us to be ladies.

Does this mean we have to sell ourselves short? Absolutely not!

It does mean that we have to be mighty comfortable in our own skin. We have to have one-hundred-percent ownership of the word *confidence.* Confidence comes from acknowledging our accomplishments, not waiting for someone else to acknowledge them for us. Oh, you betcha that it's super when someone else does, but it's a fact that all too often our achievements are ignored or simply overlooked. Gals, that's life pure and simple. We can't wait for others to give us the confidence it takes to be a real lady: we have to take control and give ourselves credit for what we can do, and we have to recognize the very real beauty we all possess.

At the same time, we have to admit that the failure to acknowledge others is not the way it should be, and, since we're women, we have the power to change it. It starts with each and every one of us. (Here comes that word *service* again.) We can take two seconds to notice a kind act and follow up with a word of recognition and praise. We must find the time to see the beauty in others when an insensitive world sees none.

Learning to serve this way may require change in the way we execute life. And change, as we've discusssed, requires courage. But courage itself feels so good when it's a constant in our lives.

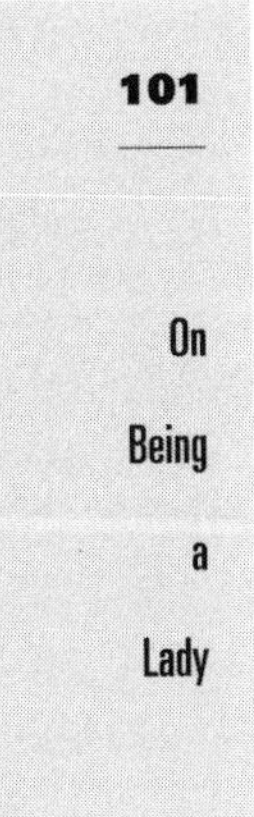

Men and women are different,
and there is no reason to think that our strength
should not be expressed in a way that is
uniquely female. If we believe that
being a lady is somehow a sign of weakness,
aren't we, in fact, rejecting the concept
that women are just as good as men?

Let's revel in our femininity,
not deny it.
If in the past you've equated
being a lady with helpless femininity,
think again.
Consider the women you know.
Among them, who are ladies?
Make a list of the characteristics they share,
and I'll bet the following words show up on it:
kind,
strong,
giving,
and powerful.

SENSUALITY:

A PASSION FOR LIVING

TO BEHOLD BEAUTY AT ANY LEVEL, to give it a place in our lives, we must be sensual, and sensuality rests in our minds. How we look at the space we occupy at any given moment. Not merely letting the moment slip by, but engaging in that moment with all our senses.

As females, sensuality is our very soul. It shows with our touch, in the way we nurture—and we are the greatest of nurturers. However, it takes training to engage our sensuality if we have been ignoring it: we must learn to succumb to our senses to become sensually aware and thereby maximize our potential as women.

I am not talking about sexuality; I am talking about sensuality as passion. Passion comes with great love. Love of people. Love of beauty, as each one of us beholds it.

The simplicity of the new-fallen snow:
Ever so quiet, sparkling clean and white,
Soft and wet to the tongue.
Each flake an artist's dream of design,
Intricate and gracefully light.

A discussion of *sensuality* inevitably leads to a discussion of *sexuality*. It can all be very confusing. Yet I have never met a woman who has not wanted to look and feel sexy at some point in her life. Sexy is really just a totally external extension of our sensuality: hair, clothes, posture, walk, the look in our eyes, the body language we emote. Sensuality, well, it's the confidence to reveal our soul, to strut our inner stuff, so to speak, and to have the carriage and attitude to pull it all off.

External sexiness doesn't last: it's a flash in the pan that breaks the ice—even melts it—but eventually it leaves us standing in the cold if it's all we've got. On the other hand, sensuality and the sexiness it fuels are steady flames that fire our hearts and warm our relationships with others.

We all know at least one woman—it may even be ourself—who isn't the photo-perfect essence of sexiness, but whom men find extremely enticing, despite a crooked nose, big ears, extra pounds. Why? Because those men are smart enough to recognize the confidence she has in herself and the sensuality/sexuality that resulted.

Women are the most intuitive beings, and our sensuality sharpens our intuition, which, in turn, sweetens our sensuality. We need to consciously foster both, because intuition backed by sensuality is the difference between right-time-right-place and missing the boat.

Some people believe that right-time-right-place is a matter of luck.

Never! We make our own luck.

Nothing is ever handed to us on a silver platter. That silver platter is earned, and we place it exactly where we want and need it to be. Let us never forget that truth, for therein lies great strength.

That strength is very heady and full of sensuality. Knowing what we want and going out and working our buns off and getting it gives us pleasure. It tickles our bones and wiggles our ears, and we radiate pleasure in a job well done: our sensual experience becomes a source of sensual pleasure to those around us.

That experience can and should be an everyday occurrence, because we are learning to find passion in all

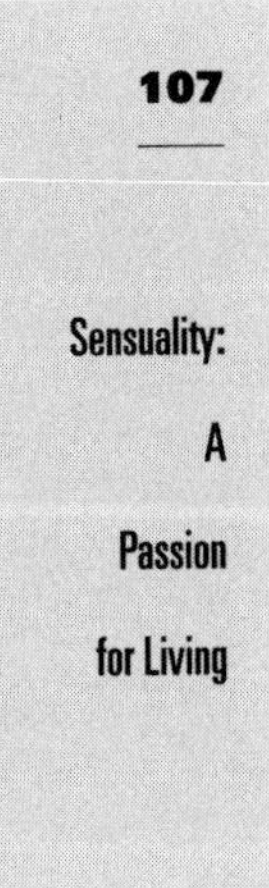

that we love and do through the play of our senses. And our senses, pardon the play on words, have always been there right under our noses.

Sometimes when things are so simple and obvious we look right past them, and, in the process, we bypass our sensuality. Why is it that we expect things to be so very complex? If we just listen and use our God-given common sense, all would be to our advantage.

Sensuality, intuition and common sense go hand-in-hand-in-hand. We positively do have a handle on this, girls. Let's use them. Let's listen to our guts. These three tools are at our very fingertips, wanting to be touched, willing and ready to be played with. Let's test our ability to use all three—sensuality, intuition, common sense—then stand back and be prepared to be amazed. We will be, again, and again, and again. Our lives will become richer and fuller with each passing minute.

Be the most sensual woman.
Believe that there is no one
With more than you have to offer.
Therein lies beauty and power and strength
and love.

It's wonderful, being a woman. We can be sensual in our relationships with all things: nature, men, women and children, with no given order. Our love has no boundaries. It's perfectly okay for us to kiss and embrace and love. In fact, it's expected. How lovely!

Tags are not bestowed upon us because we dearly hold another woman in our arms. As women, there is nothing greater than to have the love and understanding of another woman. Unfortunately, men don't always feel they're allowed this freedom with another man. Oh, sure, in sports, and as a son, father, or brother. But not as friends, and seldom in public. How dreadfully sad.

There is no greater understanding than that which two women can share. We have an unspoken, uncanny sensitivity to one another. We are not fearful of paybacks. And we understand that all our meaningful relationships have at their root an element of sensuality.

Too often, men see sensuality only as an element of their relationship with their lover: sensuality in the male mind, more often than not, conjures up images of the physical, the sexual act of intercourse.

Why, we ask ourselves
—As well as other women—
Does it so often have to come down
to intercourse?
What about the pleasure of lively
conversation
And fine-tuning gentle touches,
Holding and being held,
And simply leaving it there?

Of course, if we are fortunate enough to love and be loved by someone who encourages and believes in us and, most importantly, loves us exactly the way we are and will be, then the physical act can be inviting and exciting. But all too often men—and even some women—confuse the pleasure of shared sensuality with sex.

Sex and sensuality are both very intimate, and in the best of all worlds and relationships they're not mutually exclusive. But essentially, sex is physical and sensuality is a state of mind. We can halfheartedly participate in the former, but the latter requires a real giving on our part. That giving results in perfect moments that cannot be planned, spontaneous and mutual acts of generosity that ignite and glow between two thinking, feeling, living, breathing beings. Sometimes those moments result in the spontaneous combustion we call sex. But always they result in a communion of spirit we call intimacy.

MYSTERIES

Mystery #1: How does she do that so well?

That's the kind of question we want people to ask themselves! It puts us in the driver's seat.

It's funny how people forget how much hard work goes into a great accomplishment. (A great accomplishment can be appointment to the U.S. Supreme Court; it can also be raising happy kids.) Oftentimes, others think it comes so easy. That is because we make it look that way. We are not complaining or boasting: we are just doing and making it happen. Making our lives work for us.

This is true and honest happiness. When we are happy, then the rest of our world is happy. No amount of money in the world can buy this kind of power and happiness.

Mystery #2: How does she manage to always say the right thing?

We've already talked about being a lady. One characteristic of great ladies is that they know when to talk, and they know when to listen. And because they do more of the latter than the former, when they do speak, people listen.

So practice that aspect of "ladyhood." Revel in it, and learn to listen, then speak. And when you speak, do so with strength, and knowledge, and a belief in yourself and the value of your opinions.

Mystery #3: How does she get up the courage to ask all those questions?

Never be afraid to ask why. The smartest people make that a habit. It can never hurt, only help, and you just might learn a few tricks along the way. It will definitely help make friends: few people can resist being asked their opinion or questions about what they do or know.

Mystery #4: How does she keep from bragging about all the great stuff she does?

Ladies have great confidence, but they rarely speak of their accomplishments: they don't have to, and those accomplishments are all the more impressive when others discover them all on their own. That is part of a lady's mystery.

Mystery #5: Why is she always so happy?

Ladies love what they do, or, if they have been forced through circumstances into a less-than-ideal situation, they have made up their minds to approach it with grace and a positive attitude that inspires all around them. They focus on what is lovely and delightful and good, and, in the process of doing so, they create their own happiness.

That's part of a lady's mystery. She doesn't spend her time in talking about what she does: she simply does it. Works hard, plays hard, and is, in all, disciplined.

Mystery #6: Why doesn't she ever say anything bad about anyone?

Ladies maintain that air of mystery in the art of conversation. There is something inside them, something much of the world doesn't comprehend, that keeps them from talking about others, except in a positive way.

If you're human, gossiping is a real temptation, right up there with hot fudge sundaes and credit cards with high limits. But ladies have a real mystery about them when they resist the temptation of indulging in gossip.

They also know how to keep confidences. When someone says "Don't tell anyone I told you this," ladies take it to heart.

There is mystery in silence.
Silence about your own accomplishments.
Silence in the face of gossip.
Silence pledged to others when they confide in you.
Practice this silence, and an air of mystery
will follow.

PRAYER:

REACHING A HIGHER PLANE

BECAUSE I WAS BORN TO an Irish Catholic family, and went to a Catholic school, I went to Church.

And the Church, like the river we lived on, became a refuge from That Boy's sick cruelties.

The Church.
Peaceful and quiet.
No room for words.
No other eyes staring.
(For certainly they all know the horrible
things that are happening to me?)

The Church.
With all eyes only on the priest and the altar.
And only a loving God's on me.

The Church was the beautiful place where I discovered the strength of religion and God. I learned that God loved me no matter what, and that was the consolation I needed so much during those fearful years of my childhood.

I believe that there *is* an Almighty Significant Other to hold onto. One and the Only One Who does hear all your innermost thoughts. I wanted to be His exact likeness, female version. You ask what that means. Kind, strong, giving and powerful.

The best part is that He or She
(Whichever the case may be)
Still loves, and still believes in me,
No matter how bizarre my voice may be.

Whatever name you give the Supreme Being, I'm telling you to hang on tight to Him. That was vital to my own journey to happiness, and I think it's vital to yours, too.

So trust God. And pray.

Prayer is a wonderful way of communicating with God—and with ourselves. Nobody but you and your Almighty can hear. Prayer acts as a sounding board.

Some might refer to prayer as a form of meditation. Others might consider it a cleansing. The beauty of prayer is that we all manage to do it in as many different shapes and forms as exist among the bountiful clouds in the sky.

Prayer can be done anywhere, at any time, but we seem most inclined to pray when we are alone with our thoughts. That happens often in our hurry-up-and-wait world: we're busy, but we're alone. However, God is always there, and so those times are some of the best to pray. I like to turn off the radio in my car when I'm driving and pray for my friends: try it and see how much better it makes *you* feel.

Prayer is not a memorized verse (although it could be if that's what you desire). The prayer I'm talking about is simply good, decent, thoughts and words said privately.

Prayer can also be random acts of kindness: something done spontaneously, from the heart, that, fortunately, we're starting to hear more and more about. How lovely to know about these bursts of sunshine through life's dark clouds. It's fantastic when we're the recipient, and even better when we're the giver. (Please, let's keep them coming!)

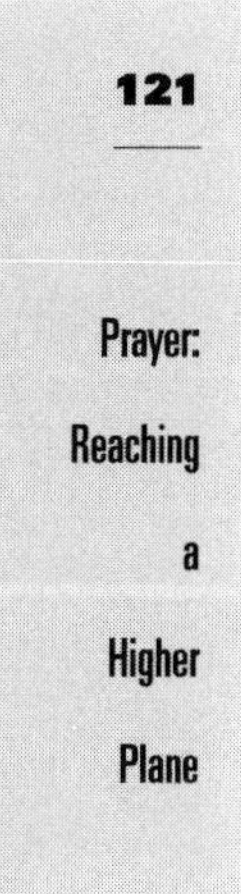

When we feel as though the whole world is coming down on us—and that happens periodically in everyone's life—prayer gives us a sense of peace, of stability and security.

When I was fourteen, I felt as though my world was caving in. Ah, the joys of adolescence and those initial encounters with raging hormones! For some reason (I don't even recall specifics now) I ran away from home. I was walking to my girlfriend's because she said I could stay there that night, when I spotted our Church in the distance and—at the very same moment—my mom in our VW bus, already out looking for me. However, I wasn't ready to go home yet, so I dropped to my belly, and did an army crawl across an open field to get to our Church. I needed that sense of peace I knew I'd find there, the security to reflect and size up my situation. Even then, prayer acted as a quality sounding board for me.

No, prayer doesn't take away the pain and make it all better, but it does give us a short breather, and hope for happier days.

Prayer may not even give us an understanding of the problem or answer the why's. Many times there are no answers. If we could see the big picture we'd have better insight, but that, friends, is the mystery of life. That mystery is where the excitement comes in.

We never know what's ahead, do we? We can lay out the best plans, and be totally on top and in charge, but only of what we have knowledge of and understand—which leaves plenty of room for the unexpected.

The element of surprise in our lives can be glorious or disastrous: it's totally dependent upon us, and who and what we surround ourselves with. We can choose to surround ourselves with positive, beautiful, upbeat people and situations, and still experience unforeseen catastrophes. How we confront them, deal with them, is the most important part of the story.

And when they are the absolutely worst catastrophes? The kind of ugly fate where we ask ourselves over and over again, "Why me?" When we've cried so long that our tears are all dried up, and we wish they weren't, because our sorrow is far from over, and we must have a way to express it. Is prayer really going to make any difference?

Yes.

All those years ago when Church was my refuge, when I prayed, "Please, dear Jesus, make it stop, make That Boy go away," and yet it didn't stop and he didn't go away—even

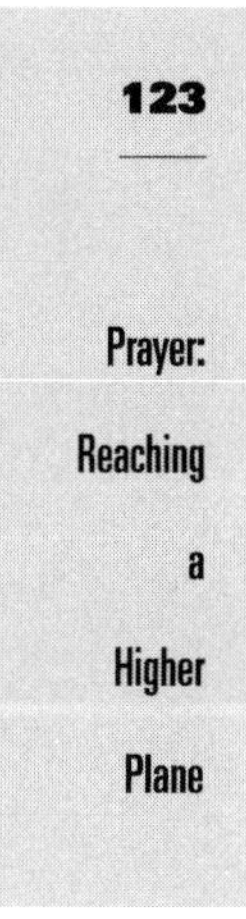

then I never gave up and I never stopped believing that one day I would find happiness.

Prayer gave me the courage to withstand and go on. And finally, as I've already related, when I was ten years old, prayer gave me the courage to tell my parents about the abuse. And they believed me. That was the turning point in my young life. Prayer was the instrument that gave me the strength, the power, the courage to reach that point and make it happen.

Whether or not you pray is your decision. But I can tell you from my experience that to fail to connect with that Higher Being willingly puts us deeper into a dungeon of despair, the black hole we know from experience gets us nowhere.

I'm asking you to believe, as I do, with whole heart and soul, that we can rise above our problems and connect with Goodness. If we look, and God knows, we have to look hard, sometimes Light prevails, even if it is just a lightening of our spirit.

Yes, I know I sound idealistic. But frankly, it works. Bottom line, belief in our beliefs and belief in ourselves is all we have. Nobody can take those things away from us, and prayer can strengthen both.

So pray, because your prayer is yours alone. And because it may just take you on a magic carpet ride the likes of which you have never experienced before.

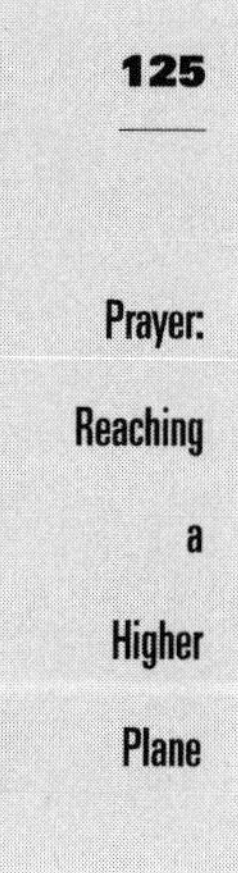

PERFECT STRANGERS.

PERFECT FRIENDS.

LAST FALL, I HAD MY FORTIETH BIRTHDAY.

My Big 4-0 was blessedly devoid of tombstones, black balloons, and that awful over-the-hill stuff.

Instead, I reveled in an abundance of love from those whom I love: I never felt that much love in such a condensed form before.

It was magnificent and intoxicating: for a whole week I was lavished with beautiful thoughts and words, visits, and cards. I was overwhelmed, on a high that was so glorious that I actually prayed that I would never have to set my feet on the ground again!

My birthday week proved to me a key point I am trying to make in this book. When we do for others in the name of love and selflessness, when our desire to serve comes from the heart, those acts return to bless us, like a huge boomerang that then lifts us, and keeps us floating on an atmosphere of love. That week, it seemed that all the love I ever showed to anyone came back to me a hundredfold.

Something else happened that week, something that brought home to me once more the importance of others in helping shape who we are.

My parents were at the surprise party that my husband, Chuck, managed to pull off, much to my embarrassment and delight. There was so much love in that room that Mom and Dad were as high as I was during that party, proud that their daughter was surrounded by such lovely friends.

That night, Mom asked me, "Joni, who taught you how to be so loving?"

I looked her right in the eye and said, "Oh, Mom, you and Dad did." "No, darling," Mom said, "your husband, Chuck, did."

She was right, you know. Through my husband's love for me, I have been able to let my love bloom and grow into the abundant, unselfish kind of love I share with others today.

Of course, that love took root in the foundation of love laid by Mom and Dad. I first learned love from them. They whetted my appetite for love. Now don't get me wrong: my parents gave me plenty of nurturing and love, much more, in fact, than the "average bear."

But for me, very likely because of the horrors of childhood abuse, it just wasn't enough.

No blame laid at my parents' feet, only thanks. Their love was so strong and true that it persuaded me to reach for more. More than that, much more than that, they gave me the gift of knowing how to love.

Love should be easy. There is a free-flowing gentleness to love. It cannot be contrived, or forced into a certain place or time. We cannot shove love into a time slot and label it "quality time."

We may be sincere in our desire to express love in quality time scheduled for seven to eight o'clock, but the recipient usually ends up feeling less than loved. We must try desperately to avoid forcing love into timeframes that are convenient for *us*. Instead, we have to be ready and willing and open to giving and accepting love anytime.

As I said before, I learned much of what I know about love from my parents and husband. But I also learned it from other people in life. Some of them friends, some of them strangers. And at every stage at which I learned, those from whom I learned were the perfect teachers for the job. Perfect Strangers, Perfect Friends.

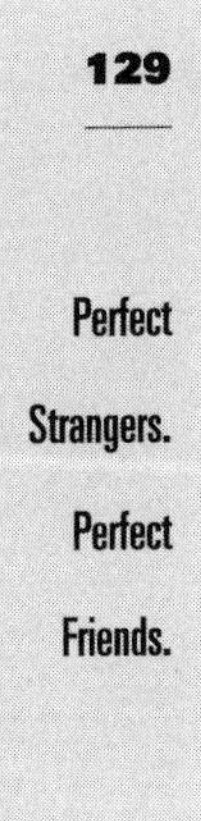

My first Perfect Friend was Peggy. I was four, and shy, pathetically shy, but Peggy was my friend.

Peggy lived on our street, and every day I went to Peggy's back door—but didn't ring the doorbell. I just stood there and waited to see if someone would notice me, this very quiet, slight, dark, curly-headed little girl. Then ever so slowly and softly I called Peggy's name, finally mustering the courage to get louder and louder until someone came to the door. Peggy was my friend, because Peggy was always glad to see me. She made me smile.

My time with Peggy was freedom from the ugliness, from being forced by That Boy to do things no child should ever even know about. Together, she and I walked to kindergarten, and played in the neighborhood. She was someone I could count on. Peggy was a comforter, a nurturer, and my very first Perfect Friend.

But, fortunately, not the last.

As I've said, I was shy at four. I couldn't look anyone in the eye, largely because of my incredible fear that the whole world knew what was happening to me.

If I was introduced to a stranger, I hid behind Mom's dress. Talk on the telephone? I couldn't call anyone: what if she didn't want to talk to me? And if she did, then what on God's green earth would I say? I literally panicked if my mother asked me to call someone for her. What if they *knew?* (I am embarrassed to say that, to this day, I still have to talk myself into making phone calls: that fear still manifests itself subconsciously after all these years, but I simply don't let it control me the way it did when I was so young.)

So you can imagine what a trauma starting kindergarten was for me. And to make it worse, my birthday was in November, so I was sent to school when I was just four. However, it was somewhat bearable because Peggy and I walked there together.

Until that horrible morning when I was running late—and Peggy went to school without me.

I froze when Mom said I had to walk to school by myself. I sobbed and pleaded to stay home, but to no avail. I was sent out into the chilly morning, and cried all the way to school, questioning where I would find the strength to walk into school late.

And since I couldn't come up with a satisfactory answer, I didn't walk into that forbidding brown building. I sat outside on the steps instead.

Eventually, the morning chill gave way to the warmth of a brilliant sun. I remember thinking that I was alone on the steps, and that the sun was alone in the sky, and suddenly its warmth flowed through me, and I burst into song, that famous song, "Somewhere Over the Rainbow." I wanted to fly with the birds it spoke of: a much lovelier fate, it seemed to me, than sitting on cold cement steps or walking into class late and being laughed at.

So I sang that song at the top of my little lungs, over and over again, and as I did, I wasn't alone anymore. I had the sun on my face, and a song that inspired my vivid imagination to take me far, far away to a place where I didn't have to deal with the terrible unknown of being tardy for the very first time.

Sometime during my third or fourth encore, as I hovered between reality and Oz, I was touched by the second Perfect Friend of my young life.

As I sang away, my beautiful kindergarten teacher came outside and stood by me. She smiled, and put her hand out for me to hold. I didn't speak, and neither did she. Somehow, she knew that I was afraid to enter my classroom. And so, from that second Perfect Friend, I learned more lessons about love.

I learned about the beauty of a woman's intuition. The comfort of touch. And the strength of silence.

I've learned so much from Perfect Strangers. From a young deaf man I met in New York City when I was still a girl, I learned patience. When I was twenty-two, Chuck and

I were on our honeymoon in Hawaii, and I was greatly inspired by the attitude of a delightful young mother I observed for just fifteen minutes as she interacted with her children: loving and laughing with them, completely immersed in the moment. She was a shining example of a warm woman and a nurturing mother. The parenting lessons I learned from that Perfect Stranger are with me yet today.

One of the greatest lessons I learned from a Perfect Stranger took place when I was thirteen and saw the movie, *Funny Girl.* I so admired the way Barbra Streisand played the part of Fanny Brice that shy, retiring, afraid-to-open-her-mouth me decided to pantomime "I Am the Greatest Star" for a special project we had at school.

I practiced for weeks. I had the costume, the attitude, the moves. And when I performed in front of my class, I brought the house down for the very first time in my life. I will always be grateful to Barbra Streisand, that Perfect Stranger, for helping me take some of my earliest steps towards overcoming those demons of shyness and shame that had plagued me throughout my young life. When I read her autobiography years later, I discovered that Ms. Streisand had her own demons to face, and acting in *Funny Girl* was integral to the process.

Years later, before I married, I met another very special Perfect Friend, whom I nicknamed Tony Tuna. But before I tell you about that wonderful man, you need to know a little bit about me twenty years ago, when I was single, living on my own.

Because I had been sexually abused, dating was scary. When I did date, I kept the relationship on the friendship level.

Guys never knew how hard it was for me to be around them in a real-date situation. I was a nervous wreck when a date walked me to my door, because that could mean a kiss. A kiss I was not ready to give. Talking came easily to me—and talk I did to get around being physical with a guy. Sometimes I wanted the hand holding and the hugs and affectionate words, but I didn't want to face the rest: too many awful memories from my childhood there. No one ever knew why, and I didn't want them to know.

Although I wasn't consciously trying to attract guys in high school, I realize now that I may have been trying to without really knowing it. I'd felt like such an ugly duckling all my life that I think that I apparently needed boys to think I was attractive, even if I didn't want them to do anything other than be enticed. Absolutely no touching! I realize now that this was my attempt to be in control when for so long as a child I had no control over what was being done to me.

Back then I wore wild clothes to camouflage what I really thought and felt. Combined with my "big hair" (when you've got curly hair like mine, you've got big hair, like it or not) and a finely-tuned dancer's physique, I had a look that appealed to males, even in high school. I learned that rather painfully one day when I was a senior.

Several of my girlfriends were going on their first-ever spring break trip to Florida, no parents. I heard them talk about it and plan it, but I was never asked to join them. It took all the courage I had, but one day I finally asked them why.

I was shocked! The reason? My "friends" hadn't asked me because they were afraid I'd steal all the boys.

Here I was, very seldom even dating any high school boys at this point, not even sexually active like my friends, and they assumed I would monopolize all the boys. It made no sense to me. And even though I knew that I could never go on the trip because my parents wouldn't let me, I was deeply hurt.

But I also learned something about love through that experience. From friends who turned out in some ways to be Perfect Strangers to me, but taught me nonetheless.

I learned that real love isn't jealous. And I vowed that day to reject jealousy at any cost. It only promotes pain and deceit, and I'd endured more than enough of that as a small child.

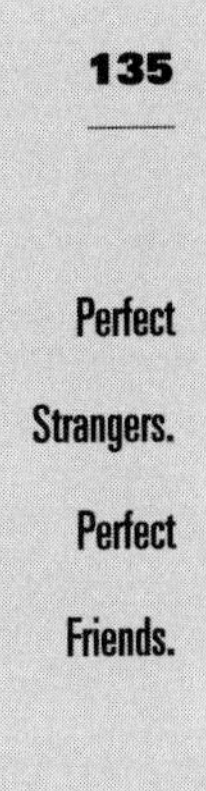

So I learned that truth about love, and I stored it with those I had learned from other Perfect Friends and Strangers along the way. But still I was haunted by nightmares of the past, and they twisted the way I approached man-woman relationships.

It was essential to me that I be in control. And I came to discover that the less I wanted from a man, the more he wanted me. I was acting more the way we think guys do: "Hey, I had a good time and you're a lot of fun, but don't call me. I'll call you." That was my way of controlling the relationship, and I reveled in it.

I was just beginning to comprehend the whole man-woman game, and to me it seemed pretty simple: don't expect anything, and you'll never be disappointed. Besides, I never wanted a man in the same way he wanted me. Why would I? It could only lead to one thing—sex—and the thought of that petrified me: I may have blocked many of the specifics of what had been done to me, but I couldn't totally forget the force, pain and deceit. I was not about to invite anything like that back into my life.

So playing it cool was my disguise. And that's where Tony Tuna finally made his appearance as a Perfect Stranger who soon became a Perfect Friend.

After high school, I took off in a VW bug with a friend, and traveled from Ohio to California. (Remember, I wanted to be a star.) However, I settled in Berkeley, not Hollywood. And instead of becoming a star, I learned some truths about men, women, and the true nature of real love. All in all, probably a better bargain than stardom.

My older sister knew some sailors who lived in Berkeley, and my friend and I moved into their house. Those sailors acted like big, gentle brothers, and they watched out for us both, which was a very good thing indeed. Our naivete was obvious to everyone but us: we, of course, considered ourselves women of the world, having traveled cross-county by ourselves via Volkswagen. From those dear, kind sailors I learned an awful lot about how nice men can really be.

Tony Tuna was one of the nicest, a true southern gentleman. He must have seen the terror in my eyes and sensed the horror in my heart when it came to a male-female relationship. So he was very patient and kind, this Perfect Stranger. He followed my lead, my slow, anguished, languishing lead. He called me his woman-child.

Yes, I was a woman-child. I hang on to this title yet today, aware of my adult emotions and passions, but keenly in tune with the child inside who was suffocated much too long. Tony made me see for the first time ever the loveliness of the meshing of adult sensuality and childlike innocence that was me.

We played together every day, Tony and I. Swam in the ocean, jumped off cliffs, walked, danced, shopped, cleaned house, played tag. Held hands, enjoyed just being silly. All the things I should have done as an innocent child.

We slept side-by-side on the floor on sleeping bags, talking till we fell asleep, holding each other, gently kissing. Slowly, I began to trust a man, this man. We were falling in love.

This Perfect-Stranger-become-Perfect-Friend taught me that love is gentle. That it shelters, protects, and never, ever bruises, or scars, or threatens. And above all, that love gives rather than takes.

I haven't heard from Tony Tuna since he sailed out of my life that summer long ago. But in my heart of hearts I know that somewhere in the world there is one very happy woman sharing her life with that gentle, dear man who taught me my first lessons about the nature of love between a man and a woman. Tony managed to give me back some of my childhood, and yet helped me begin to understand about true womanhood.

After Tony, men floated in and out of my life. And despite my experience with him, for a long time, I still felt I had to control relationships.

That was both a wonderful and horrible time in my life. I was single and broke, barely surviving on my salary as a bank teller, but always having a great time. I had several friends in the same situation, so we all took care of one another—another lesson learned about love. A very generous time those single years were.

I wasn't in touch with Mom and Dad much, not that I didn't want to be. I was growing independent and strong, and I felt I didn't belong at their home anymore. I had this sense that I had to be my own woman, no matter how tight money got, or how many cockroaches I had to kill before I went to bed. And, as much as I loved home, memories of my family and childhood brought too much of the sadness I was trying to forget, block out. I thought that if I could totally block it out, all would be well.

That worked, kind of. At least until a voice, a look, a not-so-kind man, a movie with sex and violence crossed my path. Then the terror would flood back: I could block specific memories, but I couldn't completely control the paralyzing fear. You see—in fact, you may know yourself although I pray you don't—that the trauma of child sexual abuse never really goes away. If you're blessed, thoughts of it fade. Sometimes you block it out completely: that, my friends, is how some minds and hearts survive.

Before Tony, I had a wonderful man friend who had always been just that, a friend. We used to have a ball together, and swore we'd never let our relationship turn into a boyfriend-girlfriend thing. Well, as it goes, one thing led to another, and we kissed, and then, well, maybe....

Anyway, we decided to take kissing a little farther. But suddenly I wasn't having a good time anymore. I lost it. Flipped out. Screamed, cried, shook. My poor friend had to peel me off the wall.

That was the end for me and my friend. Hard as he tried, my friend could not find the right words to console me. I was so freaked out that he couldn't even come close to me, not even touch my hand. Finally, he drove me home, and I never saw him again. Severing our friendship wasn't right, I know, but I just couldn't explain to him why I reacted the way I did.

Even though I've come to terms with the sexual abuse, there are, and may always be, situations that put me on edge, make me defensive, and cause me to go wild with terror. However, there's a difference now. Today, I don't allow my reactions to control my life the way they did for years.

It took a while after Tony Tuna, but eventually the most magnificent Perfect Stranger walked into my life. As I write this, Chuck and I have been married for nearly twenty years, and he's become the most Perfect Friend I've ever had.

Chuck's love changed forever the still somewhat cynical view I had of man-woman relationships when I met him. His love has nurtured me, and helped me grow into the woman I am today. He finished the lessons Tony Tuna started, proving to me once and for all that love is not selfish, but gives, and gives, and gives. That love is patient, always bearing with me when I'm driven by my past to strike out or retreat in fear. Chuck has taught me the healing power of selfless love, and inspired me to pass that love on to others.

That kind of love takes time. But remember, girls, that it is in our bones to love and serve one another. So look for opportunities to be a Perfect Stranger or a Perfect Friend.

When the woman ahead of you in the checkout line sneezes, bless her. Take time to stay in touch with your friends. Tell the young mother that you see with her children how beautifully they are behaving. And never fail to let your family know how much you cherish them.

Make it a habit to pay attention to all those around you and love will flow through you, unforced, easy, beautiful. And return to bless you a thousand times over.

EXERCISING

OUR OPTIONS

I STARTED MY JOURNEY TO HAPPINESS and fulfillment as a shy, introverted child in the early years of elementary school. As I told you earlier, the first step on that path came in the form of exercise.

Exercise is freedom, the freedom of movement. A sensation of letting go, unwinding. And, Lord knows, as a victimized child, I needed all the unwinding I could get.

If I was fast on my feet—which meant everything from dancing to Elvis Presley's "Nothing But a Hound Dog" to riding my bicycle far, far away to roller skating to just plain running down the hill to the river and trees—then, maybe, just maybe, **he** couldn't catch me and start the ugliness all over again.

The faster I moved, the more freedom I experienced. I was in control during those moments, although as a small child I couldn't have put that in words, nor did I know I had taken my first step on a journey to happiness. I simply knew I was free.

Quickness and swiftness of movement became a habit—or maybe a matter of survival, born out of negative experience. In high school, the sexual abuse was physically behind me, but its effects were not, so movement and its attendant freedom kept me going. I took dance classes three times a week, worked a part time job as a waitress running from table to table, and was a dancer in all our high school musicals. At the time, I never considered movement as exercise. I just knew I was making my body move the way I wanted it to and not the way I was ordered to when I was a very young victim.

Later, as an adult, I had a fitness business I loved and worked hard at for fourteen years. Why, oh why, did I choose a business full of movement? I never thought about it at the time, because I was still at a point where I was controlling my life, my body, without coming to terms with the past. I was blocking out all that ugliness: hard work for sure, but not nearly as difficult as facing the reality of what had happened to me.

However, I know now, looking back, that exercise was a lifeline that kept me afloat long enough to reach the stage in my journey where I finally could face that horrible reality. Movement was a bridge between the past and coming to terms with it.

As I told you earlier in this book, my journey may not be like yours. Mine started with externals: exercise, nutrition, clothes, good deeds. They gave me confidence, and people responded to that confidence positively. After a while, their belief in me, their approval, reinforced my confidence and sense of self to the point that when the time came, I was able to look my past squarely in the face. More importantly, I was finally able to look inside myself and begin to better develop those inner qualities of being female—muliebrity—that have contributed to the happiness and fulfillment I enjoy today.

I've already said that your path may not start with externals: I know women whose journeys were a long, quiet, inner self-searching. Once they dealt with those inner issues, the externals fell into place. I've met others who traveled a path that combined both externals and internals, hopscotching back and forth between them.

However, I am going to make a strong pitch for exercise here, not because I think we all need to look like Cindy

Crawford or Demi Moore, but because exercise empowers us. It not only gives us physical strength: it gives us energy, a sense of being comfortable in our body. And it's a wonderful way of blowing off stress.

We need to make exercise a habit, like brushing our teeth. Actually, a better analogy is flossing: for most of us that's not quite a habit, even though our dentist tells us that it should be. If we let our gums deteriorate, we lose our teeth. If we let our muscles atrophy, we lose our ability to move around freely, perhaps even our health. Most importantly, if we fail to exercise, we lose our mental edge, and miss a grand opportunity to build our confidence.

Yet many of us cringe when we hear the word *exercise.* We know it's something we *should* be doing, but most of us don't realize we need to do it consistently to reap its mental and physical benefits. And it's so darned hard to fit into our schedules.

But think, darlings. How many different things do we have to do?

Everything! As women, we are jills-of-all-trades. We can juggle twenty different activities at once—and we do.

Ah, but to juggle them with an upbeat attitude, we have to be fit. Fitness gives us an edge, keeps us sharp, helps us maintain a sunny disposition and look at ourselves in a brighter light.

"Fine for you," you may be thinking about now, "but I don't have time. How can I get up any earlier or go to bed later? You probably don't work full time, Joni." But I do, and I also have a family that counts on me. Like you, I have a schedule that never quits, but I still make time for exercise because I love what it does for me.

To fit in exercise, I sacrifice my down time. Am I missing much that way? I don't think so. After all, the day will come when I will have plenty of down time: you know, when I'm eighty-five or ninety.

Despite all my fitness cheerleading here, it's extremely important to keep in mind that *we* need to make the decision to exercise. Sure, we may get prodded by a doctor or our mate or a good friend—or even the author of a book. But we have to make up our own mind, and when we do, then and only then will we be consistent and make a habit of exercise. It will be one of the very best habits ever in the whole wide world that we'll make in our lifetime.

Exercise magnifies everything we touch, mainly because it clears our "cobwebs." If we exercise early in the morning, it helps us think through our day and our priorities.

During the day, it's an energy booster. At the end of the day, a way to release tension. Any way you cut it, it's mental therapy, and at a much lower cost than the kind you pay a psychiatrist for.

One aspect of that mental therapy is the confidence we gain from successfully forming the exercise habit: all of us should take every opportunity to instill confidence in ourselves. So please, steal that exercise time, and concentrate on the mental well-being you'll enjoy as a result, the exhilaration you'll feel because you were disciplined and followed through. You can consider the body changes a bonus.

Whatever you do, don't give up on exercise: its benefits *are* attainable if you're disciplined and consistent. And if you do occasionally slip up, simply try again and again and again. Slipping up is human nature—and it's okay. We still have the *chutzpah* to keep going.

Everyone has a different starting point, so don't compare your progress to your friends'. Don't talk about it: you'll just waste vital energy and get discouraged. Instead, take pride in staying on your own individual track. Your progress is your own: delight in every step along the way.

And no matter what your regimen, remember to smile. I'm convinced that it's the most beneficial exercise of all.

It keeps us in the right frame of mind, and it keeps everyone else guessing. *How come she's having so much fun?*

ADJUSTING OUR

FOOD ATTITUDE

OUR CULTURE HAS A LOVE-HATE RELATIONSHIP WITH FOOD.

We love to eat: just look at the enormous portions our restaurants serve up. But if we eat too much—guilt. If the doggy bag we brought home in an effort to avoid eating too much gets moldy and has to be tossed out—guilt. (Remember all those starving kids in China.) If we eat the "wrong" foods—guilt. If we go on a diet and slip—guilt. If we don't eat Mom's fat-laden family specialty at the holidays—double guilt (ours and all that Mom piles on).

If food were a man, and every aspect of our relationship with him made us feel guilty, wouldn't we begin to suspect that there was something downright unhealthy going on?

Of course we would. And it's the same with our relationship with food: it's unhealthy, both physically and mentally. So many women I know think they'd be happy and life would be wonderful if they lost weight. They refuse to live life to its fullest, always postponing what they really want to do because they think they need to lose ten pounds first. I shudder to think how many journeys to happiness have ended abruptly on a bathroom scale!

As a culture, we're obsessed with food and dieting, spending billions of dollars on weight-loss programs. Yet America is the most overweight nation in the world. So just how can we overcome this obsession, end this unhealthy emotional and physical relationship with food?

We need to adjust our Food Attitude. We have to change the way we think about fitness so it doesn't consume us. Once it consumes us, we seem to lose the power to simply make it happen.

The first step in adjusting our Food Attitude is accepting our genetic heritage. The body we own is, for the most part, genetic. Never, ever forget that. We can tighten it, shrink it, harden, soften it, but gals, love it with all your might. Stop trying to make it into something it was never destined to be.

Those perfect-body models we see are just that: models. They represent a miniscule percentage of the population. They have someone prepping them for all their photo shoots.

And they are young, so very young.

When we're that young, we believe that we need to look just like them. It will never happen. Sure, we can admire their beauty, but we should never buy into the idea that it's the only standard of beauty around.

Each and every one of us has something totally unique, something that is ours, something those airbrushed young girls will never possess. Believe it! Find what is uniquely yours and build upon it.

Don't waste your time trying to be what you're not. No matter what you do, it will never be good enough. If we're obsessed with reaching the perfect weight or fitness level, we're never satisfied. A good deal of the time that's because we're trying for a look that our body type just can't achieve.

And so we're disappointed, over and over again. We blame ourselves for lacking willpower, when it has nothing whatsoever to do with willpower.

On the contrary, I am always amazed at the willpower of overweight-underfit people who diet. Society treats these people as if they have no willpower, but that's not true. After all, they diet over and over again. Their willpower is amazing, because diets are just awful: they take incredible stamina and follow-through. (More about the pitfalls of dieting later.)

All of us, overweight or not, need to take our willpower and use it to our advantage, apply it to something that will truly help us achieve physical and mental fitness. We need to stop thinking in terms of drastic measures that leave us weak, depressed, and discouraged. Instead, we need to set achievable, moderate goals that fit into our lifestyle. (Keep in mind that lifestyles change from year to year, and when they do, goals may have to change, too.)

When we do that, we have the gratification of positive results, rather than being continually disappointed and feeling worthless. Remember, it's time for us to feel worthy.

So let's talk about diets, and why we shouldn't do them anymore. The reason lies in the word itself: diet. Die-et.

That's precisely what our metabolism does—die—when we starve it.

Our metabolism is our engine, and food is the gasoline. We must feed our body to keep it fueled and running quickly and efficiently. Food keeps our metabolism moving at a rapid pace, burning up calories. Take it away, and our metabolism drops, and begins very, very slowly burning calories. Then we go off the diet, and go back to eating normally, and our metabolic rate is still tired from being starved of fuel, and it doesn't burn all those new-found calories. What happens? We gain weight faster. Bad news.

Diets kill our basic healthy instincts. They murder our happy attitudes, and bring us to the lowest mental and physical ebb. Here we are, trying to become kind, strong, giving and powerful, and diets have the opposite effect on us. They make us weak and irritable, unable to function as the women we want to be, or they cause us to obsess about food and eat even more. Either way, we lose control of who we really are.

When I was an adolescent, I was on the Ayds candy plan, trying to do battle with my body's natural tendency to "chunk up" for the growth spurt to come. Anyway, a little piece of Ayds candy, taken with a hot drink four times a day, was supposed to suppress my appetite. Instead, I was obsessed with food: I ate everything that wasn't tied down. Sound familiar? I decided right then and there never to diet again.

We die when we *die*-t. The word says it all, so please don't do it again. Take that word and throw it out of your vocabulary like you would any other vulgarity.

Instead of dieting, let's tell ourselves to pick and choose rather than think in terms of deprivation. Let's not be a slave to food. Do we love it? Yes, we do. Does it, or will we allow it, to control us? Absolutely not.

Remember, we have total control over what we think, say and do. Our goal is to be kind, strong, giving, and powerful. Food-obsessed is not on that list: in fact, being obsessed with food—and that can mean obsessed with eating too much or eating too little—is a good way to undermine our goal.

Eating right, practicing good nutrition, was another one of those lifelines that kept me going during the years I was suppressing memories of my childhood. I believe that good nutrition is essential to our happiness, just like good gasoline is essential to having a car's engine operate smoothly. So perhaps I should be telling you all the specifics about the right kinds of food to eat, and why. I was trained in that field by the famous father of fitness and nutrition, Covert Bailey, author of *Fit or Fat.* A wonderful man, very bright and super fit in each and every way.

But you know what? You've read all the same magazines I have, seen the same television shows and documentaries, even read some fascinating books on the subject of nutrition and fitness. We've heard terrific fitness people expound on their methods of training. We all know what it's about, and still we are frustrated. And do you know why?

It's our approach, our attitude. That's why we need the new Food Attitude I've been talking about. Adjust your attitude, your mental outlook on the fitness/perfect weight craze, and you can make all that knowledge you already have work for you and quietly obtain results. We must avoid getting sucked into the waif-thin media hype. (Wouldn't it be great if those full, voluptuous Rubenesque bodies were in vogue? You can make that happen, and still be fit, beautifully.)

We also have to vow to include others in our attitude adjustment. Maybe we don't have a problem with food, but we've got problems with people who do. I was one of those people once, and I learned how wrong I was, and how much damage I was doing to the self-esteem of those I loved because of it.

When my daughter, Lauren—incredibly bright, talented Lauren—hit puberty, she began to gain weight, just as I had when I was her age. I was so obsessed with what I considered her weight problem that I couldn't see her good qualities. All I saw was that my baby girl didn't look as good as her friends. She was fat! She couldn't wear all those cute "in" clothes. So I harped and harped, and actually screamed because I was so angry with her. And so you know what all this did to my dear Lauren? That's right: she began eating even more on the sly.

Fortunately, my sister, Bethie, set me straight. One day I called her, and she asked about sweet Lauren, and all I could do was go on and on about her weight. Thank God—Bethie stopped me dead in my tracks.

"Joni," she said, "please don't do to Lauren what Mom did to me." I could hear the sadness in Bethie's voice. That was the first time I realized what Bethie had endured as a girl because she was overweight. If only she could have been judged for what she gave the world instead of what she looked like: she would feel so differently about the woman she is today. Dear, sweet Bethie: despite her accomplishments, which include being the LaLeche leader of Southwest Louisiana and raising two terrific boys, there are still ways in which she's insecure. I'm certain some of them can be traced back to the way people reacted to her weight when she was young. Of course, some of them are probably a result of her being a victim of That Boy, too. (All those years, Frannie, Bethie and I bore our pain, our shame alone: it wasn't till just a few years ago we knew we had this horrible secret in common.)

"Joni," Bethie continued, "love and praise Lauren for all the good things she does and is. Zero in on those qualities and forget the weight. The more fuss you make, the more she'll eat, just to show you who's boss. Let her know that weight does not make her good or bad or bright or stupid. It doesn't take away from her charm, her intelligence or her wit. Bite your tongue unless you have praise to offer. And don't make deals with her to lose weight."

From that moment on, I zeroed in on Lauren's gifts. I stopped giving her those side glances that said I wasn't happy about the way she looked. I softened my eyes, my voice, my thoughts.

My little girl started changing, too. As I demonstrated unconditional love, she began to feel worthy. And eventually, she decided to do something about her weight, all on her own.

It would have been okay if she hadn't decided to lose weight. What mattered most was that she had self-esteem. We can't allow ourselves to go through life thinking—about ourselves or others—that we're okay except for that extra weight. You know, that you-have-such-a-pretty-face-and-you'd-be-so-much-better-off-if-you'd-lose-that-ugly-fat approach that colors our lives and those of people around us a discouraging shade of gray. I realize now that my negative attitude towards Lauren was a whole lot uglier than fat could ever be. And we women are the absolute worst when it comes to this.

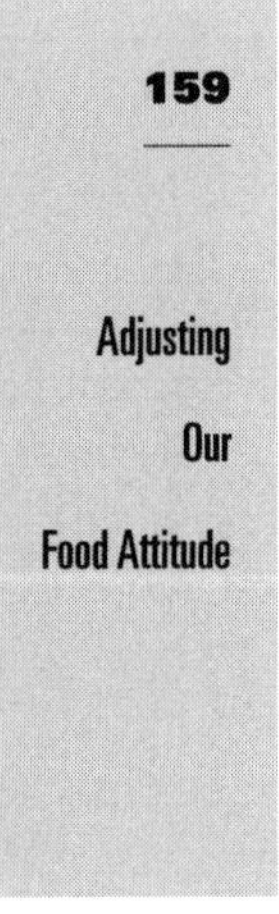

We belittle ourselves. We belittle others, if only in our minds. (How can she let herself look like that, we ask, and yet we don't know the first thing about who she is or how she got that way.) If we're that hung up on weight, if we're committing emotional murder with our thoughts, words, or attitudes, we have to stop it—right now.

However, while I don't think we should be obsessed with food and weight, I do encourage everyone to exercise and practice good nutrition. As I've said, those things helped me in my journey to happiness, giving me a sense of control and well-being that prepared me to handle steps that came further down the road. Getting in touch with our bodies through exercise and adjusting our Food Attitude can do near-miraculous things for us: I've seen it happen.

I was blessed to be a franchise owner of a Jazzercise fitness business for thirteen years. It was an unbelievably glorious business to own. All my greatest loves were mine to develop and share: music and uninhibited freedom of movement; being on stage, controlling the mood of the room; meeting perfect strangers daily; and encouraging men and women to be the best they could be.

Jazzercise was my vehicle! And boy, did I learn about myself and women in general. I used to watch women walk in the first time and hover in that back row, ready to make a quick exit. I understood, because I'd been there many times in my life, too.

So I zeroed in on every new face in a flash, doing everything in my power through my eyes, movement, and speech to make them feel as comfortable as possible—exactly what I would hope and pray someone would do for me. I knew that it took every bit of courage they could muster to get into a leotard or shorts, whatever, drive to the facility, and walk through those doors: I remember psyching myself up to come to my very first class.

If those newcomers had the determination to make it that far, it was up to me to let them know that I understood all of that. I wanted them to know that they could do it, and it was going to be okay. In their own way, they were reaching out to me, and I wasn't going to let them down. No, sir.

The miracle of it all was watching these beautiful Perfect Strangers metamorphose into the loveliest of butterflies. It was fascinating to watch the black clothing change into vibrant, self-assured, colored leotards. The moving up in line status from back row to middle, then front. Hairstyles becoming more uplifting and trendy. The very best of all was the twinkle in their eyes, that brilliant sparkle that signaled the discovery of a woman they liked being.

Beautiful, bright, airborne butterflies. It was something that happened to every one of them over a period of four to six months.

Did their bodies change? Maybe a little. But the way they viewed their bodies changed a lot. Their approach to life and themselves became clear and focused. That's what taking time for yourself can do.

Each class met twice a week consistently, religiously. We worked our fannies off together, sharing the same frustrations, laughter, melodies, and fears. Class became a safe haven for us all. As we worked out we talked about everything: I made it a point to start our dialogues with happy, uplifting issues that we as women could relate to and laugh about. It was also very important for me to be groomed immaculately: it brought forth the same response from them. We all became familiar with newfound territory together.

Well, the ironic part of all this hard fitness work is that once a month, I would bake my buns off with some sinfully delicious snack, and we, all hundred of us in each of my four classes, would gather 'round and enjoy the fruits of my labor. Once again, moderation.

What I treasure most from that time is what we all learned together—acceptance. Every one of us went through those doors the first time wanting to be a size six. Few of us got that, but that was okay. Because what we gained instead was more beauty than we could have ever imagined.

IT'S ALL IN THE

The beauty of companionship. Moderation. Learning to accept each others'—and our own—faults and differences. We learned that size doesn't dictate worth or beauty. We came to know that inner beauty gives us that outer edge we all desire, that confidence we need to make changes for the better.

Here we are again, my friends, back to the concept of change. If something isn't working in our approach to food and exercise, let's change it *now.* If we're focusing solely on outer beauty or some ideal body type, let's change the way we think by concentrating on what makes us, and others, beautiful inside. If our new approach doesn't work, let's look for another, and another, and another, until—bingo!—we discover what's working.

Courage to change. Consistency. Control. Moderation. A positive approach and disposition. They all add up to feeling-good-about-how-wonderful-it-is-to-be-a-woman. A worthy woman: one worth knowing, one worth being.

PACKAGING

AT A VERY YOUNG AGE, I discovered that dress was a way to be totally me, apart from everyone else.

Of course, it took years to be able to dress with finesse. Some of the get-ups I put together during those learning years would make your hair stand on end! But good or bad, it was still my look, solely and completely mine.

I discovered something else about dressing, too: the clothes in our closets are our costumes.

When I was a child, those costumes were my armor, a disguise; they kept people from knowing what was ticking in my mind. I found that the outward show that clothes made prevented others from seeing the *real* me: hurt, depressed, terrified, ashamed, and so painfully shy.

The way I dressed also caused others to believe I was attractive, and so they treated me as if I were, even though I felt ugly and used inside.

I wouldn't recommend anyone use clothes to cover the kinds of serious problems I faced as a child: issues like those need to be resolved, not hidden under costumes. However, through that experience, I did learn that clothes give us the ability to dress a part, reflect that facet of our personality we're in the mood to display on any given day. The way we dress can be a tremendous help when we're building on our positives to become what we want to be. To paraphrase a famous philosopher, "I dress, therefore I am."

I've said clothes are our costumes. When I think *costumes,* I think of parties. Oftentimes, gifts are given at parties. Don't you look forward most to opening the packages that are brilliantly wrapped? You know the kind: shiny, shimmering paper, tons of ribbon tied in extra big bows, with a bauble attached to tease us. We know there must be something grand inside to warrant such incredible packaging.

If we have the right attitude, life can be a party. The costumes we wear to the party of life can act as gift wrap that makes others want to know more about what lies inside. That gift wrap—the way we dress—can provide an enticing glimpse of the happy, fulfilled women we are: women worth knowing. And if we've not yet reached our goal of personal fulfillment, dressing the part—wrapping the package to reflect our dreams—can give us the confidence to continue on until we have actually become what we want to be.

So review your closet of costumes, and think of the way you "package" yourself. Make note of those clothes you wear regularly that reinforce the image you want to project. These should be comfortable, always-look-good clothes. The ones that make you stand tall, prepared to walk into any situation. The outfit with the perfect accessories. That Number Ten outfit.

Actually, I'm a firm believer that all our clothes—from play clothes to work clothes to party clothes to evening clothes to church clothes to mommy clothes to fat clothes to thin clothes to bed clothes—should all be Number Tens.

First, what we wear reflects our personality—and shouldn't that always be a Number Ten? Second, it shows Number Ten respect for the people we come in contact with. And finally, I think that first impressions last. Be honest: think about our first impressions of people. Don't we base a lot on how they look? Once that impression is in place, doesn't it take quite a bit to change it?

Fair or not, that's the way it is. So let's not take any chances: let's look our Number Ten Best at all times. It's so empowering. Have you ever noticed how much better you're treated by people when you look good? Number Ten Best demands respect!

Does that mean we have be to rich and spend oodles of money on expensive designer clothes from fine stores and exclusive boutiques? Or that we always need to wear dressy clothes?

Absolutely not! Number Ten Best has more to do with attitude and playing up our assets than money or the type of clothes we wear. Some of our most terrific outfits will come from the Salvation Army, second-hand stores, outlets, or even our best friend's closet. Number Ten Best is the way we shop, the care of our clothes, the organization of our closet. It's learning what's us, and what's not. It's lightening our load by getting rid of every scrap of clothing that doesn't package us beautifully. It's developing our own sense of style, and the confidence to carry it off consistently. We can spend tons of money and buy only designer labels, but if we fail to smile and display less-than-confident carriage, we still won't have a Number Ten Best look.

We need to remember that not everyone will agree with our style, our choices.

So what?

It's *your* image. They're *your* choices. If you feel right about them, and they're not different to the point of being offensive, don't be concerned about everyone else. Don't let a negative comment make you change what you know is right for you. When you feel good in your costume, comfortable with your style, you will automatically stand taller, more confident. People will pay attention to you, and then, like magic, your world will begin to change.

Experiment with the way you dress and wear your hair. Try on something new and different, just because *you* want to. Then go out and strut your stuff. Do it just for fun, like you did when you played dress-up as a kid. Step out of your comfort zone: remember—courage to change!

Costumes are magical: our persona changes with each one. Oh sure, the basic person stays the same: kind, strong, giving and powerful, serving others with a smile. But with each different costume our "flavor" changes, revealing a different aspect of our personality. We become what we wear.

How true. In fact, I had a personal experience that proved that to me conclusively. And if you know me, it's really pretty funny. Here goes:

As I've already related, for years, even though I was messed up inside, I had my outside act down pretty well, and that included dressing. I loved wild, vibrant, colorful clothes that at first expressed the me I wanted to be, and later, the me I was becoming.

In the early Eighties, my husband started a new business: very serious stuff, I thought. So, when faced with business entertaining, I had to—or I thought I had to—dress appropriately. Translation: boring. So I put together a businesslike wardrobe of blouses, skirts, jackets and pumps in a conservative shade of brown, which is not exactly an electrifying color for me.

And you know what? I became what I wore: boring, conservative, and dull, dull, dull. It might work for someone else, but it simply wasn't me. I just didn't feel right in those clothes, so after two or three tries, I decided to dress the way I felt most comfortable.

To my surprise, the look that best reflected me—colorful, flashy, full of movement with a touch of sexiness—increased my husband's popularity among his associates, because my clothes said that I was my own woman, and that Chuck was man enough not be threatened by that.

Clothes are powerful tools that can help us explore a range of possibilities as we work our way to personal fulfillment. Our outer costume builds our inner confidence, and as our confidence grows, it, in turn, manifests itself in costumes that are increasingly "us."

It's freeing—and it's so much fun! But it does take courage.

I was in retail for several years, and actually custom-designed clothes when I was in my thirties. So many times women came to me, wanting me to design something that really would look terrific on them, truly express who they were. And so many times, after all the fittings, all the conversations, they'd try it on for the final time—and be scared to death to wear it.

They wanted to be different, they wanted to be themselves, but they didn't have confidence when it came right down to it. I discovered that while I was designing their clothes, I also had to redesign their psyches to match. And when I did, they not only wore those clothes with confidence, but those clothes gave them the confidence to become even stronger individuals than they'd been before.

So let's gather up our courage and make a grab for the confidence that dressing Number Ten Best can give us. Let's express it—maybe even fake it a little bit at first—with a tall, confident carriage and a smile that dazzles.

Dress your outer self to reveal the beauty of your soul. Let your soul be made increasingly beautiful as it draws confidence from the way you dress. You've heard of *vicious* circles? This circle is anything but: this is a circle of growth and love. What results from it is a magical gift with an outer edge as lovely as the inner beauty it cradles.

Trust me when I say, my friends, that this wonderful gift, so beautifully packaged, can be you.

Tomorrow morning, let's all
head for our closets.
Pick out Number Ten outfits.
Put on Number Ten smiles.
Stand tall and convey confidence.
Then remind ourselves
that as we dress,
as we dream,
therefore we are.

LOOKING

IN THE MIRROR

IN THE MIRROR

I THINK THE BEST PRESENT WE CAN GIVE OURSELVES, one of the most significant stops we can make as we follow our path to personal fulfillment, is a good look in the mirror. Not for the sake of admiring the package we come in, but for a deep look into the center of our soul.

During the Middle Ages, people believed that the eyes were windows into the soul. And they were right, so very right, all those years ago.

Up till now, you may have only used your mirror to see how you look. Start using it to see how you *are.* Focus on your eyes, only your eyes; allow the rest of your image to fade into the backdrop, and pierce through to what's really important, the truth of what you feel and think.

Have you ever done this? If you haven't, you may find it's quite frightening at first, almost eerie. But we need to do it.

You know how children don't want to look you in the eye when they're lying to you or they've done something to disappoint you? When you finally get them to make eye contact, they hardly have to say a word: their eyes speak for them.

Our eyes speak to us, too, if only we let them. They tell us we're sad, even though we're desperately staying busy to avoid facing that sadness. They tell us when we're tired, discouraged, or doing things that run counter to our dreams.

But our eyes can do even more.

A few weeks ago, I was watching some championship skaters on television. Without fail, each one, right before his appearance, received a last-minute pep talk from his coach. And, also without fail, each coach delivered that talk while looking his student straight in the eye.

We can do that for ourselves. Simply by looking in the mirror and engaging in some positive self-talk.

It may sound goofy, but it works. Stand in front of your mirror, look yourself in the eye, and have a good long chat with yourself *out loud.* (I am assuming here that you're alone; try this in public and you may get some pretty strange reactions.)

Use only the most positive words in your vocabulary. Ask questions if you like, but respond with only direct, self-assured answers.

Maybe you'll ask yourself how you want others to perceive you today: be incredibly descriptive when you answer. "I want other people to think I'm strong, intelligent, charismatic, irresistible and amazing." Speak it out loud, with drama and conviction in your voice. Repeat it until it catches hold in your soul and your mind and your body and you believe it with every fiber of your being.

Perhaps you want to hurdle a fear. Tell yourself—out loud—that you will no longer *allow* yourself to be intimidated. Start with "I cans" and "I wills."

This is self-affirmation. We look into our eyes and first convince ourselves. And then we go out and convince the world. That's vital, because we get back what we give.

The world is like a mirror;
frown at it, and it frowns at you.
Smile, and it smiles, too.

HERBERT SAMUEL, ENGLISH POLITICIAN

Using the mirror this way is not some crazy idea: I do it regularly, and it works. The first time was several years ago when my husband and I got into a huge argument right before starting out on a family vacation. What was supposed to be a time of gaiety and togetherness was starting out pretty grim. And since I'd been partly responsible for that, I knew I had to do something, so I went into the bathroom and looked in the mirror for a long time. What I saw wasn't pretty. My face was angry, contorted: so that's what an argument looks like!

I began to talk out loud: "He will find me irresistible. He will find me charming. I will be bright and fun to be around. He won't be able to keep his hands off me." (When we argue, touching stops.) I looked myself straight in the eye and said it all like I sincerely meant it.

A woman I'd met once in Texas swore by this technique, claiming that the energy of the words we spoke to the mirror bounced off our reflection and energized our souls. I'm not quite sure about the scientific validity of her explanation, but it did work: I was charming, I was bright, and, trust me, Chuckie was a goner that day.

If you find that the world is frowning at you, get back to your mirror and see what's in your eyes. Chances are, you'll find you're reaping what you sow: people are simply responding to your cue.

So let's face that mirror every day, and listen to what our eyes are telling us: they are our truth serum. If we don't like what they're saying, let's change them. Let's fill them with dreams that sparkle, and with love, so that when they talk, they tell everyone around us that we're kind, strong, giving, and powerful. Let our eyes say that we've given ourselves permission to receive the best from life, and that when we do, we want to share it with others.

My best friend is overweight. In our current culture, many people regard obesity as nearly criminal behavior, just a step or two above committing ax murders. But my dear, sweet friend has encountered little prejudice and discrimination in her life, although she's large.

Do you know why? Because she never expects to be treated badly. Look into her eyes and they say, "I'm a person of worth. Respect me." She backs that up by being an excellent businesswoman and of service to all around her. Whenever we are together, I am amazed at her magnetism: people are drawn to her like bees to honey. There's no sign in her eyes that says "I'm fat: kick me." Instead, my friend gets back exactly what she puts out.

Always remember that you set the tone for your life. The pace. The pattern. In most cases, others will take your lead if it's set with conviction and kindness. In that sense, you exercise a tremendous amount of power over what you *allow* in your life.

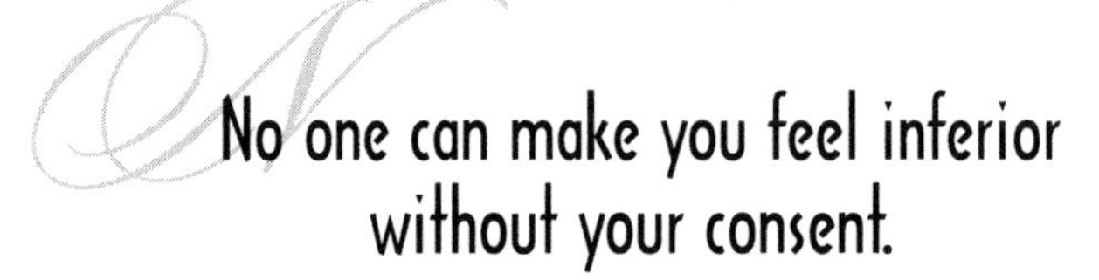

No one can make you feel inferior without your consent.

ELEANOR ROOSEVELT

Sometimes we don't know we're allowing others to treat us badly. But the second we take a look in the mirror and realize what's going on, we must stop it dead in its tracks. We must give ourselves permission to be treated well. We must embrace the power inherent in the word *allow.* Our lives are like a film: we must fully understand that we are the director, we own the director's chair, and no one—absolutely no one—has the privilege of sitting in that seat but us!

Short and sweet, what I'm talking about is attitude. A positive attitude is the ticket to life. Once you've got it, treasure it, keep it safe—heck, laminate it if you can figure out how—so that it can never become tattered or defaced.

Attitude is one thing in life that can never be taken from you. It's part of your personal style. Attitude is more important than money, jobs, education, possessions, relationships, even the roof over our heads. It can make a house a home, unite a family, make marriage a true communion of spirits.

Attitude makes things happen. I know. Because it did for me.

When I gave up my bad attitudes, my self-defeating thinking, when I locked up my past, threw it down a deep, dark hole, and tossed away the key forever, I really started to live. I began to pursue my dreams, full speed ahead. I took a look at what was good and right about me, and in turn, I began to draw out what was good and right in everyone around me. It didn't all happen at once: as you know, my journey took a long, long time, and in many ways, it continues still.

The little girl who could never smile became a kind, strong, giving, powerful woman who rarely stops smiling. The ugly duckling who was shy and awkward came to understand that she was beautiful, not just because she learned what made her look good on the outside, but because she developed the potential for loveliness that resides in all our souls, that inner beauty that causes our outer edge to radiate life.

When I began this book, I asked a question: "Why can't we all be happy?"

I'm convinced that we can, and I hope this book has convinced you, too.

May happiness be your constant companion!

It takes so much to step out on a limb.
Courage to try.
A willingness to abandon excuses.
Faith in a Power you cannot see.
Balance.
A positive attitude about yourself and
your abilities.
Discipline to make it to the very end.
And no looking back.
Only forward.

"I forgive you."

Epilogue

THIS BOOK IS A DREAM COME TRUE, a twelve-month labor of love. I wrote it because many women from all walks of life, women just like you and me, kept asking me the same question, "Why are you so happy?" As if I took a secret potion that made me that way!

So I started paying attention to my life, and did some soul-searching to find answers to that question. It was difficult to step back and take a serious look at myself, because I thought in doing so I might mess up my life somehow. I'd worked hard to gain serenity and happiness. It didn't happen by chance: good things never do.

But I wanted to make a positive difference in other women's lives, just as other kind, strong, giving, powerful women have made a difference in mine. And since I love to write, I decided to take the risk—there's the maverick in me—and put my thoughts on paper.

I'm happy to report that far from "messing it up," the process of writing this book has done nothing but make my life happier. I hope reading it has made yours happier, too.

Please write me: just a short little note or card to tell me what you're thinking. I'd like to know. Tell me about the difference you've made in someone's life, or the difference someone has made in yours. If you give me permission, I might even share it with other women in a future book or one of my presentations, and you'll make a positive difference in the lives of people you don't even know.

Above all, celebrate your muliebrity!

PERC stands for PERSONAL ENERGIES, RESOURCES, AND CAPABILITIES.

Perhaps you have someone dear in mind who you know would enjoy the messages in *Muliebrity: Qualities of a Woman*. We hope you'll take this opportunity to order one of the following items for her benefit. Please feel free to contact us at any hour, any day, at the following numbers:

TOLL-FREE PHONE ORDERS
1-888-GET-PERC (1-888-438-7372)

TOLL-FREE FAX ORDERS
1-800-286-6212

TOLL-FREE CUSTOMER SERVICE
1-888-GET-PERC (1-888-438-7372)

If one of the items you are ordering is a gift, we'd be happy to simplify the gift-giving process for you. When you order, be sure to include the name and address of that lucky person along with a few words straight from your heart. We'll enclose a gift card with the chosen item(s), and ship it directly to your Perfect Friend(s).

MULIEBRITY: QUALITIES OF A WOMAN

BOOK

192 pages of inspiration and motivation;
hardcover; illustrated. $17.95

MULIEBRITY: QUALITIES OF A WOMAN

AUDIOBOOK

Full version of the book, read by Joni.
Three tapes, runs approximately 3½ hours. $17.95

JONI'S WRITE STUFF

Beautiful note cards featuring illustrations and thoughts from Joni.
Set of 12 cards with matching envelopes. $8.95

PERC PRESENTATION

Joni's favorite thing is to be with people!
Invite her to speak with your organization of 100 or more.
Contact customer service or fax her directly at 419-531-8866.

Please know that a shipping and handling charge will be added to your order total. In addition, the required sales tax will be added for Ohio residents. We can accept VISA, MasterCard, American Express, and Discover. Sorry, no checks.

Perc Publishing

5019 DAUBER DRIVE WEST • TOLEDO, OHIO 43615 • 419-531-0088